VIRGINIA WOOLF'S *THE WAVES*

VIRGINIA WOOLF'S *THE WAVES*

BY

IRMA RANTAVAARA

KENNIKAT PRESS
Port Washington, N. Y./London

VIRGINIA WOOLF'S "THE WAVES"

First published 1960
Reissued in 1969 by Kennikat Press
Library of Congress Catalog Card No: 70-86054
SBN 8046-0634-X

Manufactured by Taylor Publishing Company   Dallas, Texas

PREFACE

This study is a sequel to *Virginia Woolf and Bloomsbury*, published in 1953, in which I concentrated on the author's personality and milieu and their influence on her art. An author's style is closely connected with his mental make-up, as Professor Leo Spitzer has indicated in his treatises on different authors' styles, but it has also to conform to the vision of a work of art, before the result is an organic whole and a successful work. My endeavour in this study has been to follow Virginia Woolf's artistic intentions and their realization in *The Waves*.

As *The Waves* is not a simple, straightforward 'story', I have considered it necessary to analyze it on the narrative as well as the symbolic level, then to proceed to see in what manner and to what extent the language employed reflects the vision and contributes to it. The language of an artist is a means of expressing an 'attitude'. Seen as an artistic activity, both its stylistic and linguistic aspects must be given attention to as equally important parts of a total structure. Thus books on grammar as well as on rhetoric have been resorted to for help in the analysis of the language and style in *The Waves*.

Mr. Leonard Woolf has kindly given me permission to quote freely from his wife's books, for which I want to thank him sincerely.

I am greatly indebted to Suomalainen Tiedeseura, Societas Scientiarum Fennica, for the honour of including this study in its series, and to Dr. O. R. Reuter, Professor of English Philology at Helsinki University and the Editor of the series, for recommending it.

My colleagues Mr. John Atkinson and Mr. Philip Binham have kindly helped me with the proofs, for which my best thanks are due.

Helsinki, March 1960.

Irma Rantavaara

CONTENTS

CHAPTER I

STRUCTURE AND PLOT

Virginia Woolf's preoccupation with the mind, the human consciousness, has a central place in all her books. In *The Waves* it is the artistic,
creative mind that she is exploring. In *To the Lighthouse* the theme had
been only an undercurrent, illuminated through Lily Briscoe's attempts
to finish her work, Mrs. Ramsay's portrait. Lily Briscoe as well as
Bernard in *The Waves* are primarily illustrative of the author's own
consciousness and method of creation, but mutatis mutandis they can
be considered to represent the creative mind in general. The account
of Lily Briscoe's manner of concentration is of special interest, for it
contains the nucleus of what is being enlarged upon in the later novel.
The description[1]) of her creative method gives a key both to the symbolism and the technique employed in *The Waves*. The importance of
rhythm is underlined, linked with the waves-imagery. 'This other
thing, this truth, this reality', which emerges behind appearances and
rouses the artist to perpetual combat, is given a fourth name: 'this
form', an ambiguous word, in keeping with the suggestive quality of
words in *The Waves*. It recalls the fact that Roger Fry and Clive Bell
were Virginia Woolf's closest friends. 'Significant form' was, undoubtedly,
a frequent theme of discussion in Bloomsbury especially when Clive
Bell and Roger Fry were preparing their collections of essays for print.[2])
The creative act in painting and writing was, as Virginia Woolf describes
in her biography of Roger Fry (pp. 239 ff.), often compared by these
friends, with special eagerness, one presumes, in the 'twenties when
Roger - Fry was busy translating Mallarmé's poetry in his spare time.
Colours play an important role in Virginia Woolf's own art; impressionism,
and even more post-impressionism, were Bloomsbury's favourite schools of

---

[1]) *To the Lighthouse*, pp. 244 ff.
[2]) CLIVE BELL, *Art*, 1914; ROGER FRY, *Vision and Design*, 1920.

painting, the latter being introduced to Great Britain by Roger Fry, against public opinion, in the first decade of this century. Thus it seems natural that Virginia Woolf should use colour imagery in *The Waves*, the interludes in particular being nothing but vivid splashes of colour in the pure impressionist manner. In a significant passage of *To the Lighthouse* Lily Briscoe is described massing her blues and umbers on the canvas, in a moment of defiance, for she had been accused of not being able to create,

> moving her brush hither and thither, but it was now heavier and went slower, as if it had fallen in with some rhythm which was dictated to her (she kept looking at the hedge, at the canvas) by what she saw, so that while her hand quivered with life, this rhythm was strong enough to bear her along with its own current. Certainly she was losing consciousness of outer things, and her name and personality and her appearance, and whether Mr. Carmichael was there or not, her mind kept throwing up from its depths, scenes, and names, and sayings, and memories and ideas, like a fountain spurting over that glaring, hideously difficult white space, while she modelled it with greens and blues.[1])

From Lily Briscoe and her struggle with art it is a short distance to Bertrand and *The Waves*.

The Waves is divided into nine sections, separated by prose-poems which describe the passage of the sun across the sky symbolizing the inevitable course of human life from birth to death. The lives of six persons, three men and three women, friends since their childhood days, are presented in chronological order through their alternating silent soliloquies. The seventh person only appears through the minds of the other six. While indirect inner monologue with its typical flash-back technique was used in *Mrs. Dalloway* and *To the Lighthouse*, in *The Waves* anticipation is predominant in the first half, retrospect in the second half of the novel. In the former two novels we have middle-aged people looking back, with the omniscient author every now and then stepping in to explain, in the latter novel 'said Bernard' (or Neville, Louis, Rhoda, Susan, Jinny) is the only direct help from the author. Structural devices are thus the more important. The process of the deepening and widening of consciousness — the theme of the novel on one level — is illuminated through the reaction to life of six different minds. In fact,

---

[1]) *To the Lighthouse*, pp. 246—7.

they form one human mind — that of Virginia Woolf, or of any other
sensitive, imaginative, creative human being. At different stages of its
development the mind reacts differently. The same sights, sounds,
experiences will at later stages turn out to have new content, according
to the mind's level of awareness and the growth of associations. A sense-
perception turns out to have symbolic meaning with ever-accumulating
implications. Reception changes into analysis, themes are collected and
interwoven. In the last section of *The Waves* synthesis is aimed at, the
leit-motifs being brought together as if in the finale of a symphony.

The symphony-metaphor, though explicitly expressed as late as on
page 182, is implied throughout the novel, a device made popular by the
Symbolists and by Proust. The structure is upheld by the help of thematic
undercurrents, which at intervals emerge to the surface, and by significant
image clusters. For example, simple ordinary happenings like 'people
passing' and 'a door opening', besides serving rhythmical purposes, are
repeatedly used as metaphors to heighten the impression of continuity,
of time passing. They aim at giving the simple story three-dimensional
width and depth, with time added as the fourth dimension. Recurrent
imagery is employed to link together the various levels of consciousness
as well as to differentiate the characters by emphasizing their individual
traits. The characterizing images are mostly very simple, almost childishly
so, being pillars to prop the canopy of symbolism. The characters themselves are 'humours', representatives of certain types on the narrative
level. On the deeper, symbolic level they turn out to be qualities in
human consciousness, which explains their marionette-like representation.
Bernard, a born 'coiner of words', 'the blower of bubbles' — these epithets
appear nineteen times in the novel — is in love with his phrase-making,
but the characters of his stories refuse to be grouped into definite
categories, for he sees people with blurred edges — a favourite expression
of Virginia Woolf's. Louis, the successful business man whose father is an
Australian banker, suffers, despite his intellectual superiority, from an
inferiority-complex because of his un-English accent. The boasting of
his school-friends remains indelibly stamped on his mind. His subconscious carries what can perhaps be called remnants of racial memory:
an echo of a savage beast stamping, and a mental picture of women
carrying red pitchers on their heads on the banks of the Nile. Neville, the
University teacher, attached to Percival who dies young, has premonitions
of impending disaster symbolized by the image of a murdered man and
the tree-metaphor. Jinny, the embodiment of sensuous appreciation of

life, appears rippling, dancing, pirouetting, surrounded with bright colours, with her frock billowing. Rhoda, like Louis, an outsider in life, incapable of forming satisfactory human contacts yet yearning for love and for the feeling of belonging somewhere, inevitably drifts towards suicide. Her personality is created by imagery conveying terror: a leaping tiger, eternal corridors, pools that she cannot cross, nightmarish dreams. The sea, waves, floating islands, sweeping swallows, deserts, form her background. Cold, innocent white is her colour, with numerous associations, one of the earliest being the white chalk that drew figures she could not understand. It seems to have drawn a circle round her, separating her from human contacts. Susan, the born mother and wife, earth-bound, untroubled by intellectual subtleties, is content with natural happiness and simple country life. Her emotions are fierce, she loves and hates with equal intensity.

The course of the six lives, covered by the nine sections, consists of early school years (section I, pp. 6—20[1])), public school (II, pp. 21—54), university for the young men (III, pp. 54—77), settling down at professions (IV, pp. 79—105), Percival's, their mutual friend's, death and the friends' reactions to the news (V, pp. 107—17), prime of life (VI, pp. 117—29), 'no longer young' (VII, pp. 131—47), friends meeting to recollect and analyze the past (VIII, pp. 149—67), summing up (IX, pp. 168—211). As a description of the human being's growth into maturity of mind the novel can further be divided into three periods, the first phase covering the school years (sections I—II) the second, from early youth to middle age (III—VII), the third, the period of growing old and looking back (VIII—IX). Yet another possibility is to divide it into two parts, before and after Percival's death.

In the first section the children, approximately between seven and twelve years of age, are at a private boarding school, Elvedon. There is neither past nor future yet, time seems to stand everlastingly in the present. The verbs in the short alternating soliloquies are also in the present tense. »'Suddenly a bee booms in my ear', said Neville. 'It is here; it is past.'» (p. 8) Vivid sense-impressions imprint themselves on the childish minds, which are mainly receptive, a mirror, a wax surface. The children are full of wonder, everything has vast proportions, hyperbole

---

[1]) The edition used is the Sixth Impression, 1950, of *The Waves*. When no name is indicated, the reference is to *The Waves*.

fits in naturally with their utterances. Impressions crowd themselves on top of each other. Synaesthesia in representation corresponds to the child's capacity of perception: water is red and hard, a look is red, words are white or yellow or fiery, warmth is yellow. Animism and personification are natural to the childish manner of thinking: purple waves are unhappy, windows are bleared eyes of blue glass, words wag their tails. They are facts, not metaphoric statements to a child.

On the first two pages, on which only sense-perceptions are conveyed, most of the important images are introduced: the loop of light, a globe hanging, the beast stamping, islands of light, the drop-image, symbolizing time. By the time the reader has reached the last section, all these images have, through repetition in different contexts, become fully illustrated. At intervals the earlier imagery is repeated, illuminated, given new dimensions. To take an example, the image of the gardeners sweeping with what to a small boy seemed giant brooms, and a lady writing, presented on page twelve as something that Bernard sees, a mere sense-perception, is later developed into a symbol of

> those enemies who change, but are always there; the forces we fight against . . . Down below, through the depths of the leaves, the gardeners swept the lawns with great brooms. The lady sat writing. Transfixed, stopped dead, I thought, 'I cannot interfere with a single stroke of those brooms. They sweep and they sweep. Nor with the fixity of that woman writing.' It is strange that one cannot stop gardeners sweeping nor dislodge a woman. There they have remained all my life. It is as if one had woken in Stonehenge surrounded by a circle of great stones, these enemies, these presences'. (pp. 170—1)

On page 202 the image is enlarged into

> those fabulous presences, men with brooms, women writing, the willow tree by the river — clouds and phantoms made out of dust too, of dust that changed, as clouds lose and take gold or red and lose their summits and billow this way and that, mutable, vain.

The willow tree, a symbol of reality in the novel, has a concrete equivalent: it is Byron's tree, 'lachrymose, down-showering, lamenting', i.e. a tree in Cambridge (p. 60). Besides it is the universal symbol of sorrow and pain, Desdemona's 'willow, willow, willow' and Neville's 'immitigable tree', 'implacable tree'.

After the simple sense-descriptions of the first pages, imagery begins to be more elaborate, undisguisedly the author's, though transferred into the childish minds. The fact that the characters use imagery which cannot be theirs at that early stage of development causes no embarrassed protest from the reader. On the contrary, there is a mysterious feeling of impending fate, caused by the fusion of the omniscient author's prophetic vision, implied in the imagery, and the childish, innocent, ignorant minds of the characters. The short, matter-of-fact statements employed to impart information and to describe facts are occasionally interspersed by flashes of imagery which correspond to the faculty of intuitive under-standing and knowledge in children, though couched in a mature manner of expression. Their seemingly casual observations concerning each other contain revealing details:

> Rhoda dreams, sucking a crust soaked in milk; Louis regards the wall opposite with snail-green eyes; Bernard moulds his bread into pellets and calls them 'people'. Neville with his clean and decisive ways has finished. He has rolled his napkin and slipped it through the silver ring. Jinny spins her fingers on the table-cloth, as if they were dancing in the sunshine, pirouetting. But I am not afraid of the heat or of the frozen winter. (p. 18)

That is Susan, aged about eight, conducting a soliloquy in her mind. Louis, in the classroom, is meditating in this unchildlike manner:

> There Rhoda sits staring at the blackboard, in the schoolroom, while we ramble off, picking here a bit of thyme, pinching here a leaf of southern wood while Bernard tells a story. Her shoulder-blades meet across her back like the wings of a small butterfly. And as she stares at the chalk figures, her mind lodges in these white circles; it steps through those white loops into emptiness, alone. They have no meaning for her. She has no answer for them. She has no body as the others have. And I, who speak with an Australian accent, whose father is a banker in Brisbane, do not fear her as I fear the others. (pp. 15—16)

The soliloquies begin to reveal the characters: Louis' loneliness, his mixture of inferiority and superiority, Jinny's generous, illusion-free, courageous though superficial nature, Susan's ambivalent emotions, Bernard's exploring mind, Rhoda's fear of people and life, Neville's analytic mind and caustic tongue.

The daily happenings at school — breakfast, classes, dinner, walking in the afternoon, evening-prayers, bath, bed-time — are given passing references, mainly through sense-impressions which imprint themselves on the mind. The buzzing of a fly on the ceiling, the shiver along the spine caused by the squeezed sponge as part of the daily bath (p. 19) are recollections vividly reproduced in Bernard's mind in his old age. (pp. 170, 205)

The development of the plot and of the characters offers the reader no surprise elements, for the clues are given at an early stage. His interest has to be kept up by other means. Flaubert is reportéd to have said to the Goncourts: 'I don't care a rap for plot or story. When I write a novel, my idea is to convey atmosphere, a nuance.'[1]) Virginia Woolf, an admirer of Flaubert and Proust, puts the theory into practice by giving the plot a place of secondary importance and concentrating on sustaining the interest through an imaginative representation of the inner and outer worlds that have to come to terms in human life. The outward atmosphere in *The Waves* is that of British upper-middle class, thus a socially limited world like Proust's, but the inner world is universal. The crucial problem on the story level would seem to be to find an answer to the question that, as Martin Turnell points out in his book on *The Art of French Fiction*, Stendhal was the first to ask within the framework of the novel in his *Henri Brulard:* What am I? — the problem of man, his existence and his responsibility and relation towards himself and others. Yet, on closer examination, this theme turns out to be of secondary importance in *The Waves*.

In the second section the boys are at a public school together, the girls at a school 'somewhere on the east coast'. Besides the daily round of school life in its place-bound, outward aspects — chapel, classes, games; courtyard with the Founder's statue, traditions attached, Headmaster's personality — significant inward happenings, common to young people anywhere, take place: there are signs of growing friendships and hero-worshipping, jealousies and antagonisms, rebellious feelings against authority of any kind, anticipations of coming joys and sorrows, widening sensibilities. Six important years, between twelve and eighteen, glide past on twenty pages (pp. 21—41). There is a suitable stop for looking back (pp. 41—52), when the last day of the last term at school has been reached. The train journey home gives an illusion of detachment, helpful in the mood of analytical valuation. A definite period is at an end. Life is waiting at the next stop. Susan feels drawn to her home in the country, Jinny to parties and pleasures, Rhoda to nowhere. For her life is a monster heaving its crest from the sea. Nameless terror is always close at hand. Louis sees himself as a link in a long chain of generations, thousands of

---

[1]) *Journal*. I. pp. 366—7. Flaubert dreamt of writing a book 'about nothing at all, a book without any external connection, and which would support itself entirely by the internal force of style' (quoted by ERICH HELLER: *The Realistic Fallacy*. The Listener, 19. 5. 55, p. 889).

years back. He himself is only 'an ephemeral passer-by, in whose mind dreams have power', a mystic with a heavy load of strange ancestral memories of sights and sounds. Bernard, vague and careless, is busy with his phrase-making. He has a mind 'like a fountain-pen ready to absorb ink', but not highly original. Neville, on his way to developing into an intellectual snob, is apt to see the mediocrity of the world rather than its loveliness. He is intelligent enough to see that he is thus losing something precious, something that simpler souls like Percival with an intuitive understanding of life possess.

Section three describes Bernard and Neville at the university, obviously Cambridge, though names are not mentioned, a fact emphasizing the significance of the inner world and the unimportance of biographical data. Louis is beginning his work in the City, the girls are settling down in life after having been to a finishing school in Switzerland. The spiritual excitement experienced by young receptive minds at Cambridge has been described by several of Virginia Woolf's friends in their memoirs and autobiographical sketches. We have them from Leonard Woolf, E. M. Forster, Bertrand Russell, Lord Keynes, and others. Virginia Woolf's description has an authentic ring, too, for though she never went to Cambridge to study, she visited her brothers there and lived in its mental atmosphere at home, Sir Leslie Stephen's atmosphere. The outward aspects of Cambridge are vividly reproduced in *The Waves:* the ancient chapels, the weeping willows on the Cam with the moon rising behind them, the Backs, the courtyards, 'the eternally joyous buildings . . . set so immemorially on the ancient turf', the punting students gliding under the bridges through 'the fountains of pendant trees', the celebrating noisy young men with their smashing of china and rollicking choruses, all the familiar sights and sounds of Cambridge student life are there. As a contrast Virginia Woolf draws Louis' world in the City: the masses of incessantly moving people, the dingy little eating-places where the clerks and other black-coated people take their modest lunches with books and newspapers propped against bottles of Worcester sauce. Louis, 'the companion of Plato, of Virgil' feels out of place there. His real life is in the 'attic room', where poetry lives, where he can contemplate eternity. Susan and Jinny continue their characteristic modes of life, the former waiting for an eligible husband to arrive on the scene, the latter enjoying being the centre of admiration. Rhoda's name-less terror increases, she is already losing her grip on life. A door opening means for Jinny a pleasant sensation of something new happening, for

Rhoda, a leap of the tiger with a whipping tongue. She feels cast up and down among people like a cork on the rough sea.

The short sentences of the previous section have been changed into longer structures. Analysis takes the place of information. Questioning begins. 'What am I? This? No, I am that.' (p. 54) Bernard, like Keats or Byron, is troubled with not finding his real self or being able to express himself. Neville, with his passion for perfection, has an ambition to become a poet, but is compelled to turn his caustic mind against himself: he is clear-sighted enough to see that he will never be any good as a poet; for all the fine words his poems sound false. By the law of attraction of opposites, Neville continues to be drawn to Percival, the Antinous-figure, the handsome athlete, who has no intellectual worries, having little subtlety of intellect. But he has character and will make a splendid representative of the mother country in India, with all his virtues of a model public-school boy and of the ordinary, games-loving, fair-playing Englishman.

In the fourth section the friends, now between twenty-two and twenty-five, are settling down in their professions. It is typical that facts concerning their lives are given in parenthesis. Facts are unimportant, it is the mind's reaction to them that matters. Metaphoric language is employed to describe even such a simple event as the arrival at a London station. 'We are about to explode in the flanks of the city like a shell in the side of some ponderous, maternal, majestic animal.' (p. 80) Bernard's engagement, mentioned in a parenthetical clause, creates in him a mystic feeling of being unmoored as a private being, traversing 'a sunless territory of non-identity' (p. 83), becoming merged into a stream of mankind, ephemeral as an individual, yet having a mysteriously pro-longed life.

The friends meet at Hampton Court to say good-bye to Percival who is leaving for India. As before, we see them only through each other's minds. The earlier characteristics are unchanged, but new nuances are added, giving new dimensions to the personalities. They are now adults — not yet twenty-five, we are told — linked together by their mutual love of Percival and their recollections of shared childhood. The approaching disaster, Percival's death, is anticipated through imagery: a dead man in the gutter, the immitigable tree, the sweeping gardeners, the tiger panting, the beast stamping, a petal falling from the rose. A red carnation in the vase symbolizes their interwoven identities. Their increased sensibility and self-knowledge are illustrated through the

intricate imagery which characterizes their attempts at self-analysis.
Their youthful expectations of happiness are contrasted by ominously
savage imagery and by the ironic juxtaposition of 'the infinite time'
before them and the premonition of death. The image of the hanging
globe, mentioned on the first page of their soliloquies as a visual fact,
now appears as a globe 'whose walls are made of Percival, of youth and
beauty, and something so deep sunk within us that we shall perhaps never
make this moment out of one man again.' (p. 104) There is dramatic and
heightened tension in this section. The fullness of life is reflected in
imagery, which suggests passion, movement, tumult, a savage joy of
life. The story has — like the lives of the people in it — reached its peak.
'The sun had risen to its full height.' (p. 105)

The short fifth section contains the news of Percival's death and the
friends' reactions to their first great sorrow.[1]) Neville's anguish is reported
in short sentences when he is trying to absorb the shock, standing with
the telegram in his hand:

> He is dead. His horse tripped. He was thrown. The sails of the world have
> swung round and caught me on the head. All is over. The lights of the world
> have gone out. There stands the tree I cannot pass. (p. 107)

He, always rebellious, feels the irony of fate. Everybody is doomed. There
is always the implacable tree that cannot be passed. Bernard's sorrow
is mitigated by the sense of continuity: a son has been born to him. One
dies, another is born, life continues. Yet he, too, finds fate cruel, 'a blank
and brutal face'. (p. 110) In all Virginia Woolf's novels the conception of
immortality is vaguely pantheistic: something remains somewhere, somehow, of a human being after his death, even if only in a few people's
memory. For Rhoda the semblance of life is made transparent through
Percival's death. She is ready for death herself.

> We will gallop together over desert hills where the swallow dips her wings in
> dark pools and the pillars stand entire. (p. 117)

The sixth section presents four soliloquies, Louis', Jinny's, Susan's
and Neville's. They are now past thirty. Louis has become a prominent
business-man, one of the Empire-builders, 'half in love with the telephone
and the typewriter', yet aware of matters of greater significance. The
attic room is still part of his life. Susan is immersed in her role of mother

---

[1]) The equivalent of this in real life, Thoby Stephen's sudden death in Greece
in 1905, is obliquely referred to on page 121: 'Percival has died (he died in Egypt;
he died in Greece; all deaths are one death.)'

and wife. Jinny continues her empty life of pleasures, but is not entirely blind to deeper issues. When the door opens, it does not any longer only mean a new pleasant sensation.

> The door goes on opening. The room fills and fills with knowledge, anguish, many kinds of ambition, much indifference, some despair. (p. 125)

She accepts life as it is, without illusions and without hope.

> I cannot tell you if life is this or that. I am going to push out into the heterogeneous crowd. I am going to be buffeted; to be flung up, and flung down, among men, like a ship on the sea. (p. 125)

The self-sufficient Neville's attempts to establish permanent human relationships have failed. He, too, has to admit the need of warmth and consolation

> for the lack of many things — I am ugly, I am weak — and the depravity of the world, and the flight of youth and Percival's death, and bitterness and rancour and envies innumerable. (p. 129)

The seventh section begins with the re-appearance of the drop-image, repeated eight times in successive sentences with an exact definition added: 'This drop falling is time tapering to a point.' (p. 131) Middle-aged, the friends are feeling the passage of life speeding up. Disappointment and disillusion, the contrast between dreams and reality, give the tone to Bernard's soliloquy. He is travelling in Italy; the leisurely existence makes him feel as if he were a convalescent, returning from stupor to life. Disappointed, he is still an eager questioner and hopeful of getting an answer one day, although his phrase-making has proved unsatisfactory in revealing the truth. Susan has found an answer to life's meaning in her children. Jinny is bravely facing the fact that she will soon cease to be attractive to men. Neville's analytic mind has helped him to become reconciled to life; he has lost something of his envy and bitterness; he is now a tolerant onlooker, dispassionate, feeling sorry for Louis and Rhoda, those 'fasting and anguished spirits' (p. 140) who want a reason for everything. Louis, prosperous, with a mahogany desk and a gold-headed cane symbolizing his opulence, is nevertheless poor, for he has lost Rhoda, the only person with whom he shared silence. He has to inhabit his attic room alone. But he thinks he has found a meaning for his existence in being a link:

> My destiny has been that I remember and must weave together, must plait into one cable the many threads, the thin, the thick, the broken, the enduring of our long history, of our tumultuous and varied day. (p. 144)

Rhoda's hatred of life is now reaching its culmination.

> There is only a thin sheet between me now and the infinite depths. (p. 146)

She longs for the union with nothingness, the only union she is capable of. She envisages her death by drowning:

> Rippling small, rippling grey, innumerable waves spread beneath us. I touch nothing. I see nothing. We may sink and settle on the waves. The sea will drum in my ears. The white petals will be darkened with sea water. They will float for a moment and then sink. Rolling me over the waves will shoulder me under. Everything falls in a tremendous shower, dissolving me. (p. 147)

The passage rings the more tragic as the author there pre-lives her own death.

Hampton Court, where the friends had earlier met to say good-bye to Percival, is the scene of the eighth section. In the course of years they have become slightly estranged, and the meeting in late middle age is something of a shock. The place is full of sad associations connected with Percival and their mutual vanished youth. Now that they have reached the mature and dispassionate vantage point of their middle age the time has come to try to interpret life and their own contribution to it. Questions are asked; the answers, if any, are given in the ninth, the last section. Has what they have made of their lives been their own choice, or has the choice been made for them? What is personality? What is the limit of human capacity of cognition? Is there a story in life and, if there is, what is it like? What is individuality worth, and what is the place of individual human life in the totality of life? The symbol of the red carnation in the vase on the table, introduced in the fourth section, is now taken up again explicitly to symbolize the oneness of the six lives. The drop-image serves the same purpose: the individual drops are dissolved into one. The fluidity of personality and, indeed, of existence is illustrated through several images: lives are streaming away 'down the unlighted avenues, past the strip of time, unidentified' (p. 161), the individual is set against 'the whirling abysses of infinite space' (p. 161), or is lost 'in the abysses of time, in the darkness' (p. 160), or set in opposition to 'this illimitable chaos . . . this formless imbecility'. (p. 160) The human being is presented in his seeming unimportance, yet every one of the friends is shown to have brought something valuable to life. Neville's contribution has been his clear and sensitive mind, which has not only been the source of the happiness he has had in life, but also of torment, leaving him exhausted. It is a mixed blessing to take 'the print of life not outwardly, but in-

wardly, upon the raw, the white, the unprotected fibre'. (p. 151) Susan's
share in life is symbolized by her rough hands, which have worked on the
land, attended to her family's needs and brought up a new generation.
Bernard has brought his phrases, unsatisfactory though they, like his
philosophy, have turned out to be in revealing the truth. Louis, a mixture
of mysticism and practicality, has added to the material wealth of the
world, which has been some consolation for his torturing vanity. Under
the cold and 'marmoreal' mask his soul has remained shivering, tender,
'infinitely young and unprotected'. (p. 155) Jinny has in her own superficial and sensuous manner brought to life some beauty, brightness and
happiness, and thus represents a positive force in life, while Rhoda is an
embodiment of frustration. In spite of her dreams of embracing the whole
world with her intuitive understanding, her real contribution has been
meagre. She does not know how to share and give and therefore condemns
herself to death as a totally useless being.

The end of the eighth section is also the end of the 'story' in *The
Waves*. The characters have been led through stages of development
from the early registering of sense-impressions to the understanding of
the common fate of mankind. The object of the last section is to draw the
conclusions and to present a synthesis through Bernard's long soliloquy.
(pp. 168—211)

»'Now to sum up', said Bernard. 'Now to explain to you the meaning
of my life.'» (p. 168) This opening of the ninth section explicitly declares
its interpretative character. Bernard becomes Virginia Woolf without a
disguise. The six lives turn out to be one life, anybody's life on one level:
biographical data are immaterial. The essential questions are everybody's
questions: what is life, what death, what personality, what reality, what
time, what truth, if any of them can be pinned down. In fact, Virginia
Woolf comes to the conclusion that they cannot. The total vision on this
level in *The Waves* is tragic, yet not negative, in spite of its evasive
attitude to, let us say, ontological questions, which are put but not an-
swered. A poet is, after all, no professional philosopher, nor is it necessary
for his success in his own *genre* to be one, provided a fresh and stimulating
approach in a satisfactory artistic form is embodied in his work. Virginia
Woolf's *alter ego* Bernard accepts the fact that very little can be known.
Truth, for him, 'immer wird, nie ist'. 'This little affair of being' remains
unsolved, 'who am I?', unanswered, human personality turns out to be an
elusive will-o'-the-wisp. Life is an unfinished phrase, stories are not true,
design in life is non-existent, language inadequate, Bernard himself a man

without a self, 'unshadowed'. Bernard's book, stuffed with phrases,
dropped to the floor, is swept up by the charwoman and thrown away
with other litter. Nothing else is left to man than bravely facing the
'perpetual warfare' of daily life and the inevitable death.

In its role of a finale, the ninth section draws together the different
elements of the previous parts. It repeats the leit-motifs and develops the
themes with their variations, such as the often-recurring 'globe' and
'willow' images, 'gardeners sweeping and the lady writing', 'the door
opening and people passing', the mind-imagery, and the 'drop' para-
phrasing, to mention some of the most important ones. Life is visualised as
having the shape of a globe, which can be turned round in the fingers and
seen in its entirety. But instead of being of solid substance it turns out to
have walls of thinnest air, fragile, dissolving into a fluid drop, which falls
when time gives it a shake. Though 'Tuesday follows Monday', life does
not seem to be susceptible to the usual descriptive treatment, which
Virginia Woolf illustrates through the image of a nurse turning over
pages of a picture-book and pointing: 'That's a cow. That's a boat.'
(p. 169) But whereas the nurse can close the book saying: 'Look. This
is the truth.' (p. 204), for Virginia Woolf it is emphatically not the
truth.[1]) The picture-book level of reality is symbolized by a willow tree
in Cambridge, the 'reality' being its transformation into 'the implacable
tree, the immitigable tree' for Neville; for Rhoda, into a tree 'on the
verge of a grey desert'; for Bernard 'that which is symbolic, and thus
perhaps permanent, if there is any permanence in our sleeping, eating,
breathing, so animal, so spiritual and tumultuous lives', (p. 176) Jinny
alone 'made the willows dance, but not with illusion; for she saw nothing
that was not there'. (p. 179) Virginia Woolf's method in the ninth section
is that of the picture-book combined with Bernard's comments on its
margin, which are his 'contribution of maturity to childhood's intuitions
— satiety and doom; the sense of what is unescapable in our lot; death;
the knowledge of limitations; how life is more obdurate than one had
thought it.' (pp. 190—1) The summary of the process of the mind's
maturing is given through a brief survey of what has been essential in
the different stages.

Recollections of Elvedon bring back to Bernard's mind the vivid
sense-perceptions: a brass handle of a cupboard glittering in the light,

---

[1]) cf. *Diary,* 12/2/1927: 'The method of writing smooth narration can't be right,
things don't happen in one's mind like that'. (p. 104).

cold water running down the body, a fly buzzing on the nursery ceiling amidst the islands of light, the taste of 'innocent bread and butter'. The child's senses are sharp and on the alert, absorbing sensations which 'happen in one second and last for ever'. Acute sense-perceptions are enlarged into a growing awareness of one's own identity: 'I am myself, not Neville, a wonderful discovery.' The next step in the development is the joining into a larger entity, a growing awareness of other people: Susan sobbing, Rhoda sailing white petals. For Bernard, the gardeners sweeping and the lady writing, Norns in an every-day setting, open up the road towards some kind of revelation. 'The virginal wax' of the six minds preserve imprints of different kinds according to their temperaments, but for every one of them childhood lays the foundation of their later development. From observing nature around them the young minds turn their searchlights to people around them: friends, teachers. It is the unnecessary detail that often incongruously sticks in their minds. So Bernard remembers the Headmaster's taut, drum-like waistcoat, Percival's flicking his hand to his neck or scratching his thigh, Louis lifting his feet like a crane, the girls looking like startled foals, a bee humming. The growing personalities with their changes of mood, youthful infatuations, jealousies, fears, vanities — enigmatic, haughty, formidable Louis, precise, caustic, extremist Neville, vague, sociable, ever-changing Bernard, now Hamlet, now Shelley, Dostoevsky, Byron, 'but mostly Byron' — are seen by the ageing Bernard in half-tender, half-humorous light. Eager, curious youth changes into the mechanic attitudes of later life, the rapturous young love into the interminable breakfasts of married life.

> 'Pass' . . . I would say. 'Milk' . . . she might answer, or 'Mary's coming' . . . — simple words for those who have inherited the spoils of all the ages but not as said then, day after day, in the full tide of life, when one feels complete, entire, at breakfast. (p. 185)

Despite the growing feeling of failure and disappointment, Bernard feels that life has been worth living: he has been part — even if an insignificant part—of a magnificent spectacle: Life. Death can be faced with equanimity.

> Again I see before me the usual street. The canopy of civilisation is burnt out. The sky is dark as polished whalebone. But there is a kindling in the sky whether of lamplight or of dawn. There is a stir of some sort — sparrows on plane trees somewhere chirping. There is a sense of the break of day. I will not call it dawn. What is dawn in the city to an elderly man standing in the street looking up rather dizzily at the sky? Dawn in some sort of whitening of the sky; some sort of renewal. Another day; another general awakening. The stars draw back and

are extinguished. The bars deepen themselves between the waves. The film of mist thickens on the fields. A redness gathers on the roses, even on the pale rose that hangs by the bedroom window. A bird chirps. Cottagers light their early candles. Yes, this is the eternal renewal, the incessant rise and fall and fall and rise again.

And in me too the wave rises. It swells; it arches its back. I am aware once more of a new desire, something rising beneath me like the proud horse whose rider first spurs and then pulls him back. What enemy do we now perceive advaɴcing against us, you whom I ride now, as we stand pawing this stretch on pavement? It is death. Death is the enemy. It is death against whom I ride with my spear couched and my hair flying back like a young man's, like Percival's, when he galloped in India. I strike spurs into my horse. Against you I will fling myself, unvanquished and unyielding, O Death.' (pp. 210—11)

On closing the book after concentrating on the surface story, the reader is left with a feeling of admiration for the ambitious effort of the novelist. But some lack of complete satisfaction is also felt: the pieces of the puzzle have not yet been put in their places to make a satisfactorily coherent whole. Thus, as a novel proper, *The Waves* falls short of perfection. The content of a novel like *The Waves*, an extended metaphor, is, however, naturally not exhausted by the unravelling of the plot, however close the reading may be. It is, above all, as the autobiography of a mind that *The Waves* maintains the reader's interest.

CHAPTER II

SYMBOLISM AND IMAGERY

Several interesting interpretations have been worked out centering round symbolism in *The Waves*, the most illuminating being by Peter and Margaret Havard-Williams[1]) and by John Graham[2]). The author herself wrote in her *Diary*, after the publication of *The Waves:*

»What I want is to be told that this is solid and means something. What it means, I myself shan't know till I write another book. And I'm the hare, a long way ahead of the hounds of my critics.»[3])

---

[1]) *Bateau Ivre: The Symbol of the Sea in Virginia Woolf's T h e W a v e s.* English Studies 1953, Vol. 34, Nos. 1—6, Amsterdam-Bern-Copenhagen; pp. 9—17.

[2]) *Time in the Novels of Virginia Woolf.* University of Toronto Quarterly, Vol. XVII, 1948—9, Toronto, pp. 186—201.

[3]) *Diary*, 22. 9. 1931, p. 174.

The business of the artist is to suggest, not to explain.[1]) In the following *The Waves* is being considered on its level of suggestion and seen as an autobiography of a creative mind, an exploration into the forces that are combined in, and necessary for, the creative work of an artist.

The workings of the mind had been an object of interest and study for Virginia Woolf ever since *Jacob's Room* (1921). *The Waves* is no deviation, it is a continuation of the same theme of which different variations had been practised in *Jacob's Room*, *Mrs. Dalloway*, *To the Lighthouse*, *A Room of One's Own*, and *Orlando*. In these earlier works she had concentrated on unravelling more or less 'ordinary' people's minds. In *The Waves* she attempted the most complex task of all: to probe into the secrets — secrets even to the owner of the mind herself — of an artist's, in this case a writer's, consciousness. As is natural, Virginia Woolf's favourite authors were those who are also concerned with this theme: Shakespeare, Montaigne, Sir Thomas Browne, Sterne, the Russian writers, De Quincey, Proust, the Symbolists. She was among the first to recognize the significance of *Ulysses*, while it was still in progress of appearing in the *Little Review*.[2]) The Hogarth Press had published translations of the psychoanalysts' works, which undoubtedly added to her interest in, and intuitive knowledge of, the deeper layers of the mind. But she was no imitator of either Proust or Joyce, nor of Freud or Jung. Though at the mention of her 'philosophy' she would probably with self-irony have referred to Bernard's, which, 'always accumulating, welling up moment by moment, runs like quicksilver, a dozen ways at once' (p. 155), there is a constancy of vision, based on feminine intuition rather than intellect, in her manner of looking at the world around her and, especially, within her. With matter having lost its solidity and becoming energy, with time, personality and mind having changed their accepted characteristics, she did not consider herself justified to write novels in the old-fashioned manner. »I shall be right to go along this very lonely path», she wrote to E. M. Forster a little pathetically[3]), lonely, despite Proust and Joyce, for she saw man as

---

[1]) To read difficult poetry, Virginia Woolf says in *The Waves*, 'one must have myriad eyes. One must put aside antipathies and jealousies and not interrupt. One must have patience and infinite care and let the light sound, whether of spiders' delicate feet on a leaf or the chuckle of water in some irrelevant drain-pipe, unfold too ... And so ... let down one's net deeper and deeper and gently draw in and bring to the surface what he said and she said and make poetry.' (pp. 141–2.)

[2]) cf. *The Common Reader* I, p. 190.

[3]) *Diary*, 16. 11. 1931, p. 176.

an *animal symbolicum*, living in a symbolic universe which, for her, was
reflected primarily in language and art, excluding e.g. religion. Ibsen, in his
later plays, and the French Symbolists are more relevant points of comparison than Proust and Joyce, for all their preoccupation with the mind.

The imagery that Virginia Woolf uses to illustrate her conception
of the mind conveys that she sees it functioning both like a mirror
and a lamp, i.e. both as Plato's passive reflector and as Plotinus' active
projector.[1]) It is 'the virginal wax', 'our white wax', on which sensations
leave their imprints. It bears resemblance to the *camera obscura* of Locke
in that it is a kind of container.

> Rich and heavy sensations form on the roof of my mind; down showers the day
> — the woods; and Elvedon; Susan and the pigeon. Pouring down the walls of
> my mind, running together, the day falls copious, resplendent. (p. 19)

The surface level slips along, like a pale-grey stream reflecting what
passes (p. 81), or is like a lake unbroken by oars. (p. 26) A mixture of
passiveness and activity is conveyed by the image of a fountain-pen
filled 'with whatever happens to be the contents of a room or a railway
carriage' (p. 49), or with imaginary pictures (p. 57). In a moment of
revelation the mind becomes overfilled. 'The sweetness of this content
overflowing runs down the walls of my mind, and liberates understanding.' (p. 116) The moment of vision implies an active element, too,
but the visionary manner of seeing is the result of passive waiting for
the right moment.

> Something lies deeply buried. For one moment I thought to grasp it. But bury it,
> bury it; let it breed, hidden in the depths of my mind some day to fructify.
> After a long lifetime, loosely, in a moment of revelation, I may lay hands on it,
> but now the idea breaks in my hand. (p. 112)

The mind is frequently presented as contributing to the creation of the
object of perception: the willow tree changes its appearance according to
the onlooker. (p. 60) In its active role consciousness throws out streamers;
it is characterized by swiftness and rhythm and must not be disturbed
in its activity. It probably conveys something of Virginia Woolf's own
visual imagination that she speaks about 'the horrible activity of the
mind's eye' (p. 187), a torment to its owner.

Virginia Woolf is in many ways related to the great romantics. Here
Wordsworth and Coleridge offer the most obvious objects of comparison
with their ideas of the mind as 'creator and receiver both, / Working but

---

[1]) cf. M. H. Abrams, *The Mirror and the Lamp*, pp. 23, 58 ff.

in alliance with the works / Which it beholds.'[1]) The reader is frequently reminded of *The Prelude*, although Wordsworth's diction and imagery are studiedly simple — though often the result defeated the aim — and his text is comparatively bare of similes, metaphors and parallelisms, which are Virginia Woolf's special stylistic helpmates. Both *The Prelude* and *The Waves* are *Bildungsgeschichte* in the sense that they proceed from the simple sense-perceptions of a child to higher levels of consciousness.[2]) In Wordsworth's *Immortality Ode*, another illustration of the growth of the human mind into maturity[3]), there is an image, that of a tree, which Neville's 'immitigable tree, implacable tree', symbolizing death, Angst, carries an echo of. In Wordsworth's *Ode* the tree-symbol is left open, unexplained, but its obvious meaning points to something ominous, inevitable, comparable to death or doom. In Rossetti's *King's Tragedy* the symbolic content of 'a shadow-plant', 'a black yew-tree' is self-evident.

Coleridge's ideas concerning consciousness and the content and working of the mind, which in his opinion always contains a current of the past and an impulse towards continuity, must have aroused Virginia Woolf's interest, although there is no mention of them in her *Diary*.

> »How opposite to nature and the fact», says Coleridge, »to talk of the 'one moment' of Hume, of our whole being an aggregate of successive single sensations? Is not every one at the same moment conscious that there co-exist a thousand others, a darker shade, or less light?»

Coleridge also speaks about 'the streamy nature of associations which thinking curbs and rudders.' Continuity is expressed in innumerable images with Virginia Woolf. Time for her always contains an antithetical element. Things happen in one second and last for ever. She puts in juxtaposition the limited time of the clock and the unlimited time of the mind.

---

[1]) *The Prelude* (1850 ed.) II, pp. 257—60.

[2]) Faulkner's *The Sound and the Fury* can be included in the same category, widely different in the application of the theme though these three books are. Faulkner's range is pitched much lower, between the mature but limited and simple mind of a negro servant and the under-developed consciousness of an imbecile, who only knows *how*, and even that deficiently, but not *why*. Wordsworth's and Virginia Woolf's characters are highly civilized, contemplative, capable of analysis. Despite the difference in the material of the three works, the process of achieving mature acceptance of life is their mutual theme.

[3]) Coleridge speaks of Wordsworth's attempt to reach »the twilight realms of consciousness», and of his interest »in modes of inmost being to which ... the attributes of time and space are inapplicable and alien, but which yet cannot be conveyed save in symbols of time and space». (*Biographia Literaria*, p. 268).

Her imagery concerning time is particularly rich. On page 131 the word
'time' is repeated seven times in different images. The most recurring of
them is that of a drop falling, repeated eight times on that page alone.
The corrosive effect of water and the dwindling of time are being
associated (cf. later p. 55). Yet with Virginia Woolf time has a two-way
movement: it diminishes in the form of a spiral, as with Proust, yet it
also enlarges itself into infinity, again as with Proust. The conception
of 'the unlimited time of the mind, which stretches in a flash from Shakespeare to ourselves' (p. 194) places consciousness outside space and time,
making it an everlasting *now*. It is a constant flux

> — a rushing stream of broken dreams, nursery rhymes, street cries, half-
> finished sentences and sights — elm trees, willow trees, gardeners sweeping,
> women writing — that rise and sink. (p. 181)

The unity of content and form is implied: structure, plot, symbolism,
technique, rhythm are all in embryo embedded in that passage.

The wave-symbolism pervades all the layers of the novel, horizontally
as well as vertically, in imagery as well as rhythm. In *The Voyage Out* and
Jacob's Room the sea had already played a minor part. It had an important role in *To the Lighthouse*, the spiritual biography of Virginia Woolf's
parents, which through its very theme came naturally to be associated
with the happy childhood summers at St. Ives accompanied by the sound
of the sea. For her the waves gradually came to acquire ever-widening
associations, romantic, mythical, even psychological. Freud, Jung,
Ferenczi, e.g., have pointed to the mythical role of the ocean as the
ultimate source of life, a symbol of 'das Ur-Mutterliche'.[1]) Further, Freud
speaks about the 'oceanic' sensation of being at one with the universe.[2])
The imagery of *The Waves* has also obvious affinity with Freudian
thought concerning the subconscious. As an artist Virginia Woolf put
great reliance on the subconscious workings of the mind in the process of
creation.[3]) The sea is employed to symbolize that layer of the mind out of

---

[1]) cf. F. O. Matthiessen *The Achievement of T. S. Eliot*, pp. 136 ff., and C. A.
BODELSEN, *T. S. Eliot's Four Quartets*, p. 36, on Eliot's sea symbolism; also EDMUND
WILSON's interpretation of symbolism in Dr. ZHIVAGO, The Encounter, June 1959,
pp. 5—16.

[2]) Virginia Woolf's suicide by drowning has something of the symbolic in it:
in Freudian jargon, she returned to the safety of her mother's embrace, of which she
was deprived when she was thirteen. It was after her mother's death that she had
her first nervous breakdown and attempted suicide.

[3]) There is an important passage on this theme in *A Room of One's Own*, pp.
145—158.

which rise sudden glimpses of illumination, flashes of vision. Coleridge's corresponding images were similarly those of movement, effects of light: the sun dispersing mists, rays of moonlight, flights of birds, leaves in the wind, etc. He speaks about 'the unfathomable depths of Shakespeare's oceanic mind'. Both in Virginia Woolf's *Diary* (D) and in *The Waves* (W) there is a particularly tenacious image of motion, that of the fin of a fish. A fin turns (W p. 134), or rises out of the wastes of silence and sinks back into it (W p. 194), a flashing fin breaks the waste of the immeasurable sea (W p. 201), a fin breaking a leaden waste of waters (W p. 174, D p. 169), a fin cuts the green glass of a lake (W p. 130), a fin passes far out (D p. 101). It is significant that the waters referred to are 'leaden wastes', 'a green glass', 'silence', i.e., at rest, undisturbed. The happy moment of a sudden vision is not at one's beck and call, the waters have to be calm, 'leaden', inert.

The waves do not, in *The Waves*, serve the content only, they are also an integral part of the form, determining the rhythm of the novel. It is the ebb and flow, the rhythmical motion of the surge that reflects itself in the main stylistic devices, repetition, accumulation, and antithesis. The sentences grow and move like waves: figure is heaped on figure, there are eddies and undercurrents, rollers and swelling surges.

> '*The Waves* is, I think', Virginia Woolf writes on August 20, 1930, 'resolving itself (I am at page 100) into a series of dramatic soliloquies. The thing is to keep them running homogeneously in and out, in the rhythm of the waves. Can they be read consecutively? I know nothing about that. I think, this is the greatest opportunity I have yet been able to give myself; therefore I suppose the most complete failure. Yet I respect myself for writing this book, yes — even though it exhibits my congenital faults.' (D p. 159)

This is a piece of clear-sighted self-criticism, not uncommon in Virginia Woolf's *Diary*, and one of her endearing traits. However, before the author and the novel had reached that point of sureness, a long period of painful trial-and-error development had preceded. The *Diary* allows the reader to follow the process of artistic creation at unusually close quarters. It is the more interesting as in *The Waves* Virginia Woolf was a thoroughly conscious artist and a skilled craftsman who was trying to 'write out her mood as it came to her' like Byron in *Don Juan*. Their theme, too, was on the surface level the same: life and human personality, but treated in a widely different manner. Virginia Woolf, like Byron, wanted to put everything in, yet to retain only the essential, to combine deliberate creation with reliance on the subconscious. The process was full of strain, as we see from the *Diary*.[1])

On the surface level *The Waves* is a chronological story stretching from childhood to old age, subjected to the modes of thought: time and space. On the deeper level, that of human consciousness, time can be presented as amorphous. The happenings in consciousness have the same irrationally ever-changing field of movement and shifting time as they have in sleep. On the story-level the problems of life, death, reality, and personality remain unanswered, but on the symbolic level they turn out to have another content and become integrated into a meaningful whole. It now becomes clear why the author wanted to create, as she writes in the *Diary* 'in a very few strokes the essentials of a person's character. It should be done boldly, almost as caricature.'[2]) The characters are not primarily meant to be personalities[3]), their main role is, as I see it, to represent components of the mind, the powers needed for artistic creation. They are thus unchanging qualities and, needing allegorical presentation, can best be drawn through recurrent images, 'in bold strokes'. Allegory, as Rafael Koskimies points out in his book on poetry[4]), is a poor substitute for symbolism which, if happy, is adequate as such. Digging up allegorical 'meanings' only detracts from the value of a work of art, it may justly be said. Yet, in my opinion, in *The Waves* allegory adds to the richness and significance of the novel, being effortlessly subjected to the symbolism of the work and thus an integrated part of the whole, not a disturbance, nor necessarily a weakness.

In the following an attempt is made in this light to trace the dominant features of the different characters in order to see what contribution and illumination this treatment would give to the vision of the author. Bernard is here, too, seen as the central personality, an artist whose creative work is assisted and made possible by the forces represented

---

[1]) A more detailed discussion on this subject is included in my paper on *Romantic Imagery in Virginia Woolf's T h e   W a v e s*, Bulletin of the Modern Language Association 1 LX 1959 Helsinki, pp. 72—89.

[2]) *Diary* 9. 4. 1930, p. 157.

[3]) There is an interesting passage in the *Diary*, written October 5, 1931, after the appearance of the earliest reviews on *The Waves*: »I wonder if it is good to feel this remoteness — that is, that *The Waves* is *not* what they say. Odd, that they (The Times) should praise my characters *when I meant to have none*.» (p. 175) [the italics are mine.]

[4]) *Yleinen runousoppi*, p. 111.

by the other characters. Percival[1]), the man of action, represents
normality in its most gentlemanly and laudable aspects.

> Being naturally truthful, he did not see the point of these exaggerations, and
> was borne on by a natural sense of the fitting, was indeed a great master of the
> art of living so that he seems to have lived long, and to have spread calm around
> him, indifference one might almost say, certainly to his own advancement, save
> that he had also great compassion. (p. 111)

Percival is necessary for the story as a background, an object of the
different reactions, in the same way as the willow tree, a symbol of reality
and of sorrow, is an object. Percival dies young: he has fulfilled his task
in the novel as a human being, but he continues to be necessary as an
ever-present memory in Bernard's consciousness. The fact that there are
an even number of women and men represented in the story recalls Virginia
Woolf's theory of the best creative minds having to be androgynous,
an idea taken up from Coleridge[2]). What it means is that there must take
place a fusion of the male and female elements of the mind, 'a marriage
of opposites', before it is fully fertilized and able to use all its faculties.
Shakespeare, Keats, Sterne, Cowper, Lamb, Coleridge and Proust are
quoted as examples. (Emily Brontë could have been added to the list.)
With *Orlando*[3]) and *A Room of One's Own* in mind, it is perhaps not too
far-fetched to consider the different characters of *The Waves* in this light.
Susan and Jinny would embody the sensuous and sensual elements in the
human psyche. Susan represents on one hand the duty-bound instinct
which makes people marry, beget children, toil in daily work, in general
'making the world go round'. On the other hand she can be seen as a
symbol of the blind basic instincts of hate and love. According to this
interpretation Jinny symbolizes the life of the senses at their full vigour
and gaiety adding to harmony and happiness in life. In this light the
colour and movement symbolism with which she is characterized is
revealed with a new suggestiveness. Neville is the embodiment of intellectual pursuits, needed for furnishing a background for the artist's work
and a spur to perfection. Louis and Rhoda represent the deepest layers

---

[1]) The name may be a coincidence but it is suggestive of the knight in the Grail-
legend, especially when in the novel Percival's magnificence is compared to that of
»some mediaeval commander» (p. 26).

[2]) and enlarged upon in *A Room of One's Own*, pp. 146 ff.

[3]) Orlando, we remember, is a writer who changes his sex after some 200 years
of his life. In several ways *Orlando* is a forerunner of *The Waves*, although in the
former the theme is treated in the manner of a phantasy.

of the human mind, the region of the unconscious. It is true that similari-
ties with Jung's doctrines of archetypes and of racial memory can be
seen in Louis' characteristics, but ever since antiquity the working of
inspiration and its secret sources have been the natural object of artistic
speculation. It is not necessary to tie *The Waves* too closely to any
fashionable psychological doctrines. Especially Rhoda is an original and
ingenious embodiment of, and is drawn with, artistic insight. Bernard
himself, besides being the central figure, the sum total of the different
elements, can also be understood as representing a particular aspect: he is
the conscious craftsman, busy with his note-book, on a constant hunt
for the right word, phrase, and image, revising and rewriting, feeling
desperate and elated in turn, 'eternally engaged of finding some perfect
phrase that fits this very moment exactly'. (p. 50) Byron, Tolstoy,
Dostoevsky, Meredith lend features to his early attempts at writing.

That the 'hero' of *The Waves* is Bernard's mind, one single consciousness, is illuminated by several images. In the important fourth section,
where the friends meet to say good-bye to Percival, the symbolic red
carnation, then seven-sided, is introduced, 'a whole flower to which every
eye brings its own contribution'. (p. 91) In section VIII, when they meet
again, it has become a six-sided flower. Their unity is characterized also
by their representation as six instruments making up an orchestra, six
slices of one cake, six fishes in the sea, the sea symbolizing the flux of
consciousness. Throughout the book Bernard gives clues for this interpretation by repeatedly pointing out that there are many Bernards, that
he is not one and single but complex and many, made up of several
components. The question, Who am I?, instead of being left open as on
the narrative level, is given many-sided illumination on this symbolic level.

In his highly interesting book on poetry[1]) John Press, himself a poet,
illustrates (backed by wide acquaintance with relevant material, e.g.
analyses by leading poets of their own manner of artistic creation), how
a poem grows beneath the surface of the poet's conscious mind, how it
takes its origin

> from the promptings of his animal sensibility, from his response to the images
> and rhythms that present themselves to him and from his ability to transmute
> all his experiences and memories into poetry. This work of sifting, refining and
> condensing the divergent elements that constitute the flux of being is largely
> unconscious, and the foundations upon which a poem rests lie hidden and sub-

---

[1]) *The Fire and the Fountain.* An Essay on Poetry. Oxford University Press
1955.

merged beneath the deep waters of the poet's mind. It would, however, be a grave mistake to depreciate the importance of the conscious, deliberate crafts-manship that goes to the making of a poem. (p. 232)

T. S. Eliot in *Tradition and Individual Talent*[1]) also refers to the fusion of different elements in the act of creation. *The Waves* is Virginia Woolf's argument to the same effect.

The fourth section is particularly revealing for this argument. The sun is at its zenith, the lives of the characters are in their prime, their personalities fully shaped, their faculties at their most vigorous. Structurally this section is exactly the middle of the book, dividing it into two parts: anticipation changes into retrospect. At this point time is standing still, it is a moment of suspension. Consciousness is on the alert for an important event: Percival's arrival, i.e. the moment of artistic conception. 'Things quiver as if not yet in being.' (p. 85)[2]) Bernard is in the mood for introspection and exploration. He is conscious of the perpetual stream of consciousness, the surface of which reflects what passes, the sensations, but he is also aware of the activity below the surface. It arouses his interest and wish

> to exercise my prerogative not always to act, but to explore; to hear vague, ancestral sounds of boughs creaking, of mammoths; to indulge impossible desires to embrace the whole world with the arms of understanding — impossible for those who act. (p. 82)

He is proudly conscious of his powers — a propitious mood for creation — and conceives himself called upon to provide a meaning for all his observations, 'a line that runs from one to another, a summing up that completes'. (p. 83) The characters are in this section first presented as seen by each other. Neville, excited, sees Louis enter, a mixture of assurance and timidity; Susan is, as usual, likened to some animal, here to a wild beast who moves as if by instinct, stealthily, yet assured. Rhoda slips in unnoticed, tortured, because snatched from her dream-world. Jinny, colourful, rippling and flowing, bringing in new sensations, becomes the centre of attention. Bernard is seen by Neville as one who half knows everybody yet knows nobody. But they all need Percival for their existence:

> — without Percival there is no solidity. We are silhouettes, hollow phantoms moving mistily without a background. (p. 87)

---

[1]) *The Sacred Wood*, p. 55.

[2]) See a corresponding description in *A Room of One's Own*, p. 157.

His arrival means stirring up the components of consciousness, the creation of necessary tension. He arouses the elements needed for artistic
conception. Childhood memories are recalled, each one of the friends
connected with characteristic imagery. Bernard's memories centre on
sense-impressions: water running down the spine, the gardeners sweeping,
the lady writing; Susan's, on associations with passion: the boot-boy
making love to the scullery-maid; Rhoda's, on terror: the tiger panting;
Neville's, on feelings of Angst: the dead man in the gutter, the immitigable
tree; Jinny's, on aspects of joy: a dancing leaf; Louis', on the sense of
isolation: a lonely corner in the garden. Their memories are balls of string
which they unfurl when they come together. They all bring their
contribution to the common hoard.

> Exposed to all these different lights, what we had in us (for we are all
> so different) came intermittently, in violent patches, spaced by blank voids,
> to the surface as if some acid had dropped unequally on the plate. (p. 90)

The imagery attached to their different personalities is illuminative of
interacting layers and powers of consciousness. Bernard cannot bear
solitude; without his friends he is nothing. His phrases have value only
if helped by the others. He is the good mixer, the observer, the curious
mind, the explorer who furnishes the material and does the polishing
up, but the others are indispensable in giving substance and content
to what he says. Louis, with his thousand lives and the sound of songs
on the Nile and the chained beast stamping, carries, as pointed out
above, Jungian connotations of the collective unconscious and of racial
memory. He is the primitive, Neville the civilized element, both necessary
for the poet: Louis represents the depth where the roots of poetry lie,
while Neville is the merciless intellect cutting like a rapier. Susan,
'debased and hide-bound by the bestial and beautiful passion of
maternity' (p. 94) is only capable of feeling the primitive emotions of
love, hate, rage, and pain, but her contribution is important, as poetry is
concerned with the whole man, body as well as soul. Louis admires
Susan and Percival, those two who are in harmony with their unconscious:
a woman relying on her instincts, and a man of action who is not
concerned with artistic creation, yet possesses an intuitive understanding
of life. Louis finds himself a slave working for Neville and Bernard,
'the caged tiger, and you are the keepers with red-hot bars' (p. 92).
Louis is conscious of his power, 'yet the apparition that appears above
ground after ages of non-entity will be spent in terror lest you should
laugh at me . . .' (p. 92), all images with Freudian connotations. Jinny

asserts her friendship with Louis: sensuality in harmony with the unconscious, Neville retains 'the splendid clarity and the remorseless honesty' (p. 61) of his mind, though attracted by Jinny and troubled by his frustrated desire for her for a time.

Rhoda is the most interesting of the characters and the one most lovingly drawn. On the level of personality-description there is in her a combination of features that are part of Virginia Woolf's own mental make-up, its highly-strung, nervous, schizophrenic side, undoubtedly important for her as an artist. Rhoda represents the neurotic element of Virginia Woolf's — or any artist's, psyche[1]), while Bernard is representative of her sanity and of her happy immersion in the occupation of an artist. But besides the aspects of personality with its autobiographical interest, Rhoda can symbolically be seen as the indispensable but elusive helpmate of every artist: intuition and inspiration. Rhoda's portrait combines the irrational forces of the human psyche, the mysterious elements which are the truest source of inspiration. Both Louis and Rhoda have their roots in the unconscious. As early as on page eight Louis is characterized by one of the recurrent two-level images that typify him:

> Up here my eyes are green leaves, unseeing. I am a boy in grey flannels with a belt fastened by a brass snake up here. Down there my eyes are the lidless eyes of a stone figure in a desert by the Nile. I see women passing with red pitchers to the river; I see camels swaying and men in turbans. I hear tramplings, tremblings, stirrings round me. (p. 8)

Later on 'up here' also means 'the attic room' as the opposite pole of the depths of the unconscious, the ideal and the primitive linked together. Similarly Rhoda is characterized as moving on two levels: 'I am the foam that sweeps and fills the uttermost rims of the rocks with whiteness; I am also a girl, here in this room.' (p. 77) Rhoda is the feminine element, Louis the masculine — they are lovers, but Rhoda's elusiveness and fear make their permanent relationship impossible. Rhoda must be free to come and go, she is an Ariel, unfettered, who must remain 'outside the loop of time', in emptiness, alone. She has no face, her body lets light through, she floats in the air and is wafted down tunnels.

> I have no end in view. I do not know how to run minute to minute and hour to hour, solving them by some natural force until they make the whole and indivisible mass that you call life. (p. 93)

---

[1]) cf. MARGARET AND PETER HAVARD-WILLIAMS' interpretation of her as an embodiment of a frustrated artist, *art.cit.* pp. 9—17.

She is

> like the foam that races over the beach on the moonlight that falls arrowlike
> here on a tin can, there on a spike of the mailed sea holly or a bone or a half-
> eaten boat. I am whirled down caverns, and flap like paper against endless
> corridors, and must press my hand against the wall to draw myself back. (p. 93)

The will-o'-the-wisp quality of inspiration is happily caught in the imagery.

Her other roles as the embodiment of the struggling irrational forces
in the depths of the unconscious — the death-wish, sexually tinged
romantic dreams (p. 41), the defiance and the wish for power (the
Empress-dream on p. 40), the inexplicable feelings of terror — become
repeatedly illuminated through imagery. The frequent appearance of the
colour white is characteristic — the field she observes is white with
daisies, her ships are white, so are the petals which, as a child, she used
to float in the basin, or the foam she identifies herself with. White is a
generally accepted symbol of loneliness, innocence, melancholia, 'of
infinite remoteness tinged with bewilderment', says John Press[1]), a definition applicable to Rhoda-symbolism, too. Rhoda's melancholia results in
suicide by drowning. Inspiration, having finished its task, vanishes into
the sea of the unconscious. Sea-imagery is specially connected with
Rhoda. The threatening monster, life, heaves its crest from the sea, with
long waves pursuing her. She is in constant terror.

> The door opens; the tiger leaps. The door opens; terror rushes in; terror upon
> terror, pursuing me. (p. 75)

Her happiness is made out of solitude and silence, of existence in the
dream-world.

> Pools lie on the other side of the world reflecting marble columns. The swallow
> dips her wing in dark pools . . . The moon rides through blue seas alone. (p. 76)

For Bernard the meeting of the friends at Hampton Court is a moment
of 'ravenous identity', of 'egotistic exultation' (p. 102), that is to say, a
moment of fullest intensity in the process of creation, corresponding to
Lily Briscoe's flashes of vision in *To the Lighthouse*. The globe-image
becomes invested with new content: it is here a symbol of full, ecstatic
experience to which the different elements in Bernard's consciousness
bring their contribution. The globe is said to be made of 'youth and
beauty', 'of Percival', i.e. memories, 'of seas and jungles', 'of the howlings
of jackals and moonlight', 'of ordinary happiness', 'of week-days', all
epithets connected with the different personalities.

---

[1]) *op.cit.*, p. 162.

In the second half of the novel Virginia Woolf concentrates on deciphering the workings of memory. It is difficult for a modern writer to take up this theme and avoid Proustian imitation. His influence is unescapable, but both Virginia Woolf and Faulkner have proved that it need not be a shackle. Brooding upon the past, evoking childhood, the most formative years in a poet's life by general acceptance[1]), recalling past experience and trying to interpret its meaning, are the leading themes in the latter part. An emotionally important event like Percival's death is buried deep in the recesses of the mind, making itself felt in many fruitful ways. In the course of life different kinds of experience are being collected. Another meeting at Hampton Court, in the eighth section, gives the opportunity of seeing to what extent human consciousness has been able to digest the material collected. While the minds have matured and become enriched through actual experience, the sensibilities have lost something of their youthful sharpness and eagerness. But what has been lost in intensity, is being offset by deeper, maturer insight into relationships and aspects of life. Neville's share, the intellectual attitude, has grown. Tolerance and dispassionate judgment have taken the place of intuition: Rhoda is preparing for her suicide. Susan's and Jinny's illusionless realism has given them satisfaction, whereas Bernard's technical skill has proved inadequate. Louis is in vain trying to bridge the ideal and the real, the attic room and the City, E. M. Forster's 'outer world of telegrams and anger'. Sensibilities have grown dull, there is only the life of habit left, of one event following another.

> Knock, knock, knock. Must, must, must. Must go, must sleep, must wake, must get up — sober, merciful word which we pretend to revile, which we press tight to our hearts, without which we should be undone. (p. 166)

The summing up is Bernard's, the artist's, attempt to fuse together the different elements and to force a pattern upon chaos. The deepest meaning, he finds, has been in 'those moments of humiliation and triumph that come now and then undeniably'. (p. 169) Bernard's attitude to his task as an artist is one of ambivalent oscillation between hate and love, but it is the very tension that means life at its fullest. He is not a Tonio Kröger, a writer with a guilty conscience. The tension is not between art and life. The pursuance of art is one of the modes of the 'good life' that the Bloomsbury group were concerned with. The struggle for artistic perfection is 'good life' at its best. Bernard's attitude is undoubtedly

---

[1]) *ibid.* pp. 196—7.

Virginia Woolf's own. When planning and writing the end of *The Waves* she wrote in her *Diary* on December 22, 1930: 'The theme effort, effort dominates: not the waves: and personality: and defiance.' (p. 162) The insistence upon defiance recalls Lily Briscoe's perseverance in adhering to her own manner of expression. Bernard's riding with his spear couched against death illustrates on the symbolic level the artist's constant struggle with his art. Life and art become fused into one in *The Waves*.

CHAPTER III

LANGUAGE AND STYLE

1. GENERAL[1])

Language and style are determined by the artist's vision, by what Wolfgang Kayser calls Haltung, the attitude.[2]) Virginia Woolf's 'attitude' in *The Waves* is to apprehend experience, catch it 'in the raw', and convey it as direct as possible, through language. Words, their associations and connotations, the technical devices employed, including rhythm, are to be made to correspond to the happenings inside the mind. The artist's development is a process from one intensified state of consciousness to another.

> 'Look', said Rhoda; listen. Look how the light becomes richer, second by second, and bloom and ripeness lie everywhere; and our eyes, as they range round this room with all its tables, seem to push through curtains of colour, red, orange, umber and queer ambiguous tints, which yield like veils and close behind them, and one thing melts into another. (p. 96)

The Waves is characterized by such figures as repetition, parallelism, accumulation and hyperbole, all four specially contributing to the feeling of intensity. The moment of vision is intuitive, not analytical; the happenings inside the mind are fragmentary and irrational. Impressionism with its dominant features of ellipsis, suggestion, split syntax, its stream-of-consciousness method, reflections of sense-impressions, and numerous other devices, are made use of perhaps to as great an extent as in any

---

[1]) See the Introduction in *Style in the French Novel* by STEPHEN ULLMANN for a survey of the development of stylistics. Its notes and bibliography cover a wide range of the field and serve as an excellent source of reference.

[2]) W. KAYSER, *Das sprachliche Kunstwerk*, p. 292.

novel in world literature. But *The Waves* is also an expression of a vision, an evidence of a subjective attitude. Allegorical and symbolic presentation with its preference for 'types' instead of living characters is among the expressionistic attitudes employed. By blending impressionism and expressionism the author creates a shifting angle of vision, with the outer and the inner worlds becoming fused. The *now* reigning in consciousness, stretching to cover the past, the present, and the future, as opposed to the instantaneous *now* of the phenomenal world, is evoked by means of thematic imagery, the associative use of the language, rhythmical devices, e.g. the use of the ing-forms, or the shifting use of the tenses, the past tense denoting something habitual and the historical present tense used for things past.

Virginia Woolf is in *The Waves* a virtuoso in her handling of the language, a word-magician, which is an attitude apt to put off many a reader who does not care for the word-juggling that is displayed in this novel particularly. But for anyone interested in the problems of language and style *The Waves* offers a many-sided illustration of what language can be made to do. For Virginia Woolf, as for every artist, words exist to suggest rather than to state. She wants them to retain their dynamic, metaphoric element.[1] For her, words 'uncover', 'draw the veil off the things'. She wants to invest them with the dynamic quality of the Greek Logos, with being and becoming involved, both preserving and revealing, in Heideggerian language, 'das sagbare Seiende', 'die ursprüngliche Wahrheit'. The process from sign to symbol can perhaps be seen as being comparable to that from perception to concept-forming, characterized through what Yrjö Reenpää calls 'eine Zeitenthebung'.[2] Symbol is transferred to the plane of timelessness.

The experience illustrated in *The Waves* is dominated by the senses and the 'now; this moment in June', but it becomes 'zeitenthoben' in the *now* of the combined past-present-future of consciousness. It is time-bound, yet timeless. Virginia Woolf's ambition seems to concentrate on

---

[1] RAFAEL KOSKIMIES in his *Yleinen Runousoppi*, p. 105, agreeing with Cassirer, Stenzel and Pongs, refers to the metaphoric element as the basic quality of language. SUSANNE K. LANGER, basing her theory of art on that of Cassirer's emphasis on 'symbolic forms' speaks about 'the mythic conception of words'. *Feeling and Form*, p. 131.

[2] REENPÄÄ, *Aufbau der allgemeinen Sinnesphysiologie*, p. 83: »Schlagwortig kann gesagt werden, dass das Seiende der Begriffe eine Zeitenthebung aus dem im zeitlichen 'Jetzt' befindlichen, in der Aktual-Zeit Seienden, dem Empfundenen ist.«

stretching the manner of expression to reach even further than Proust, who employed the novellistic, descriptive technique in conveying his inner world of things past yet ever-present in memory.[1]) There is no denying that Proust's world is much wider in significance than Virginia Woolf's. His private consciousness is both a microscope and a telescope, imprisoning minute impressions as well as nebulae emanating from disintegrating society.

Virginia Woolf wanted to 'de-novellize' the novel, as Chekhov, whom she greatly admired, had de-dramatized drama, and T. S. Eliot was de-poetizing poetry. Only, Chekhov had gone, and Eliot was going, in the opposite direction, from ornate language to outward simplicity in vocabulary and expression (though there was plenty of complicity involved in connotations and ambiguity). All three would prefer silence — Mallarmé's 'significant silence' — or at least expression condensed in the extreme. They point out that there is no language for the deepest human emotions. Mystics resort to silence, lovers to 'little language', 'broken words, inarticulate words, like the shuffling of feet on the pavement'. (p. 16) Speech is false; a cry, a howl is needed, Virginia Woolf says, thus stressing the affective, what linguists consider to be the primary, function of words.[2]) Virginia Woolf discarded simplicity in expression and proceeded to the other extreme, to suggestion by word-magic, as it were, in the manner of a Keats, a Gerard Manley Hopkins, or the Symbolists rather than that of an Eliot. She broke the frontiers of the novel stepping over in the direction of lyric poetry while Eliot was proceeding from poetry to prose. Virginia Woolf was led to the attempt by her nature as much as by the Zeitgeist, for she lacked the quality of an epic writer, as can be seen especially in *Day and Night* and *The Years*, which are interesting exactly in the points where the author deviated from the usual novellistic writing. She is clearly a lyric poet *manquée*, by nature 'ein stark lyrischer Dichtertyp oder eine für das lyrische Erlebnis besonders empfängliche Seelenstruktur'[3]), a type whose characteristics, according to Koskimies, specially consist of an innate tendency towards living in a moment and creating an illusion of timelessness. This is exactly what Virginia Woolf is trying to do, especially in *The Waves*. The excess of

---

[1]) MARTIN TURNELL calls Proust a writer with a multiple vision, »master of all techniques», *op.cit.* p. 13.

[2]) cf. e.g. OTTO JESPERSEN, *Language*, p. 424, or LAURI HAKULINEN, *Sanojen sanottavaa*, pp. 21 ff.

[3]) KOSKIMIES, *Theorie des Romans*, p. 59.

metaphors can be seen to derive from an attempt to convey the timeless, flux-like happenings in human consciousness by means of 'zeitenthoben', metaphoric language.

Virginia Woolf's interest in her medium appears in the frequency of discussions on the topic scattered all over her works, novels as well as essays. In her essay on *Craftsmanship*[1]) and in *A Letter to a Young Poet*, in the same collection of essays[2]) she has the theme for special consideration. Words are for her something fragile, light, elusive, likened to butterflies, balloons, bubbles. They are not to be commanded. The irrational, underground element in the writer's work is laid emphasis upon. A semantic interest is a natural ally to the 'mythic' conception of language. The art of writing means for Virginia Woolf the art 'of having at one's beck and call every word in the language, of knowing their weights, colours, sounds, associations, and thus making them, as is so necessary in English, suggest more than they can state . . .'[3]) She is related to the romantics in her demand for intensity in the author to carry off the reader into an ecstatic rather than analytic reception of the work of art. Like Keats, she finds 'fine excess' necessary in poetry and relies on brief moments of revelation rather than on sustained but un-inspired evenness of writing — the 'sustained effort' that E. A. Poe, too, found so little merit in. Intensity is also T. S. Eliot's key-word, but his reference is to analytical intellect as much as to emotion. Virginia Woolf's language aims at lulling the mind into receptiveness, not waking it up to critical analysis. Both writers emphasize the importance of continuity and certain historicity in the language of poetry as well as of prose. These two qualities together with 'boldness' and variety are what Virginia Woolf lifts up for special recommendation in her advice to a young poet. She reminds him that in every poet there live all the poets of the past. *Orlando* offers an illustration of these tenets. So does *The Waves*.

In *The Waves* the expression and what is being expressed fall in with each other: the stylistic devices also serve to illustrate the stream of consciousness. Thus, for instance, echoes and quotations from earlier writers — a device which both Eliot[4]) and Virginia Woolf use to enrich their own writing — also correspond to

---

[1]) Broadcast on April 20, 1937, published in *The Death of the Moth*, pp. 126—132.

[2]) *Ibid*. pp. 132—144.

[3]) *Craftsmanship*, op. cit., p. 142.

[4]) ELIOT took the method of using quotations from Ezra Pound. In *The Waste*

the rushing stream of broken dreams, nursery rhymes, street cries, half-finished sentences and sights — elm trees, willow trees, gardeners sweeping, women writing — that rise and sink even when we hand a lady down to dinner. (p. 181)

In *The Waves* (p. 41), Rhoda goes into the library, takes out a book and reads a poem about a hedge. There are no quotation marks and no names are mentioned, but a closer reading reveals that the poem must be *The Question* by Shelley. 'Green cowbind and the moonlight-coloured May, wild roses and ivy serpentine' come straight out of stanza III, 'the river's trembling edge . . . the water-lilies broad and bright, which lit the oak that overhung the hedge with moonlight beams of their own watery light' are lines 1, 4—6 of stanza IV, almost unaltered. Rhoda's soliloquy ends with a rhetorical question 'Oh.' to whom?', which are the last words in Shelley's poem. Shelley's language melts into Virginia Woolf's without any noticeable break in her style. Both use epithets in profusion and like to heighten the effect with hyperbole and visual imagery. 'Radiant with million constellations, tinged / with shades of infinite colour, / And semicircled with a belt / Flashing incessant meteors' comes from Shelley's youthful *Queen Mab*, but the quotation could easily be fused into Virginia Woolf's text in *The Waves* without being noticed as a quotation. There is great affinity between Virginia Woolf and the romantics in general.[1])

Shakespeare is the obvious source to go to for associations, for not only does his mastership in ambiguity fit in well with Virginia Woolf's conception of language, but his presence, unconsciously or consciously, in every cultured Briton's mind is a natural background for echoes. Snatches from Shakespeare float in Bernard's mind. 'But I am not afraid of heat, nor of the frozen winters' (p. 18) recalls the song from *Cymbeline* (quoted also on p. 12 in *Mrs. Dalloway*). Percival's death becomes linked in the reader's mind with Hamlet's by a simple associative sentence: 'No lullaby has ever occurred to me capable of singing him to rest.' (p. 172) 'Come away, Death' appears in two passages (pp. 184, 200). 'Let me not to the marriage of true minds' (p. 184) is the first line of Sonnet XVIII. Other easily recognizable sources have been used too. 'The lily of the day is fairer in May' (p. 188) comes from a poem by Ben Jonson. The

---

Land there are allusions to, and adaptations of, thirty-five different writers, and passages in six foreign languages, including sanskrit, according to C. M. Bowra, cf. *The Creative Experiment*, p. 163.

[1]) See further on this theme my *art. cit.* Bulletin of the Modern Language Association, 1 LX 1959, Helsinki, pp. 72—89.

four-line poem beginning 'O, western wind, when wilt thou blow', repeated in broken snatches, floating in Louis' mind (pp. 143—5) is by an anonymous 16th-century poet. The frequent references to 'little language' recall Swift. Nursery rhymes are being mixed with snatches of poetry, reflecting the content of the stream of consciousness. (pp. 184, 200)

Individual words are employed to give colour and tone. *Multitudinous*, with its Shakespearean and romantic echoes, causes an anti-climax when used in a banal connection.[1]) Other words that have Shakespearean, archaic and romantic connotations are, e.g. *sere*, *supernal* (Poe had used both of them), *cozen*, and *fell*. *Fell* is used four times, with shifting nuances of content: »Susan's head, with its fell look . . .» (p. 30); »cold as lead, fell as a bullet . . .» (p. 64); »What I give is fell . . .» (p. 71); » . . . how fell, how entire Susan's glance is . . .» (p. 102). According to OED, *fell* is now only used poetically and rhetorically in the meaning 'cruel, savage, ruthless, intensely painful, destructive'. It is specially connected with Susan, whose sympathies and antagonisms are indeed fierce. She, typifying das Ur-Weibliche, the savagely protective mother with the primitive feminine instincts, is tersely described through this archaic word. It has romantic undertones too: Shelley uses it in *The Revolt of Islam*, Canto II, stanza 4: »The land in which I lived, by a fell bane / was withered up.» In Wordsworth's *Prelude*, line 318: »I was a fell destroyer», it appears in the 1805—6 version, but has been deleted from the 1850 version, perhaps because of its quaintness, as Wordsworth was aiming at what he considered 'natural' diction. Milton had used it in its form 'felon'. Henry James, in his *Portrait of a Lady* speaks about 'these fell Europeans'.

Like *scrolloping* (p. 31)[2]), *brim* is a neologism: »Yours (your eyes) grow full and brim and never break». (p. 11) According to OED, *brim* is still used in northern dialects meaning 'fierce, stormy, rough, raging'. The context here would, however, suggest a melting together of its obsolete meaning 'brilliant, shining' and 'brimful', full of tears. Dryden speaks of 'her brimful eyes', so does Burns, in the meaning 'full to the brim'. With Shakespeare 'brimful' appears four times. Keats has 'brimfull of their friendliness'. By using 'brim', Virginia Woolf creates an enriching ambiguity: when the eyes are full of tears they are also shining.

---

[1]) 'Multitudinous, carrying attaché-cases, dodging with incredible celerity in and out, they went past like a river in spate.' (p. 198.)

[2]) Cf. chapter on the ing-forms, p. 84

The vocabulary of *The Waves* is extensive, ranging between the colloquial and the unusual, the latter including poetic and archaic words, of Gallic, Greek, French, Latin, and Anglo-Saxon origins. The following examples have been chosen to illustrate the quality of the loan-words:

assagai (or assegai) (pp. 54, 78, 100), 'a slender spear', is a Berber word of Portuguese origin. 'Men with assagai' is connected with imagery where movement and primitive emotions are involved.

Words of Latin and French origin, from zoology:

guillemot (p. 67). 'They dive and plunge like guillemots whose feathers are slippery with oil.'

gizzard (p. 112). It is not an uncommon feature with Virginia Woolf to have a prosaic word in a highly emotional context. Here Bernard's agony is being described after the news of Percival's death have reached him, and he is sitting in the Italian Room of the National Gallery trying to find some consolation. »I doubt that Titian ever felt this rat gnaw. Painters live lives of methodical absorption, adding stroke to stroke. They are not like poets — scapegoats; they are not chained to the rock. Hence the silence, the sublimity. Yet that crimson must have burnt in Titian's gizzard.»

prehensile (p. 67). The picture created is both humorous and graphic: »Supple-faced, with rippling skins, that are always twitching with the multiplicity of their sensations, prehensile like monkeys, greased to this particular moment, they are discussing with all the right gestures the sale of a piano.»

Words of Greek origin:

deleterious (p. 56), used in an unusual combination: 'his bold and deleterious figure'.
encaustic (p. 29): 'Jinny always dances in the hall on the ugly, the encaustic tiles.'
panacea (p. 148): 'There is no panacea (let me note) against the shock of meeting.' A pompous word in a colloquial context.
proboscis (p. 132): The learned-sounding Greek word with its prosaic meaning is used mock-solemnly, as often with Virginia Woolf: 'Could I prolong this sense another six inches I have a foreboding that I should touch some queer territory. But I have a very limited proboscis.'

'Unnecessary' Gallicisms[1]) and Latinisms are frequent:

envisage (p. 80); 'Men clutch their newspapers a little tighter, as our wind sweeps them, envisaging death.'
purview (p. 98): '. . . pale shadows on the utmost horizon, India for instance, rise into our purview.'
purlieu (pp. 17, 18): 'I will use this hour of solitude . . . to coast round the purlieus of the house . . .'

---

[1]) cf. H. W. FOWLER, *A Dictionary of Modern English Usage*, pp. 144, 784.

circumambient (p. 82). Here, too, a pompous word in a ridiculous situation adds to the humorous effect: '. . . invent a purple lady, circumambient, hauled from the barouche landau by a perspiring husband sometime in the sixties.'

eviscerate (p. 177): 'Then there is the being eviscerated — drawn out, spun like a spider's web and twisted in agony round a thorn.' Discrepant images are boldly linked together.

Words like *insensate, lugubriously, meretricious, oleaginous, sedulous,* etc. would be replaced by other adjectives and adverbs in spoken English. There is no attempt to make the silent soliloquies sound normal speech, although colloquialisms are included. They are intentionally mixed with the stylized and elated expressions, making the language reflect the shifting angle of vision.

In general, the vocabulary is composed of both short, Anglo-Saxon words and longer Latin-French words. On analysis, it is somewhat surprising to note that the short Anglo-Saxon words predominate. It is the stylistic devices rather than elaborate words that give the language of *The Waves* its ornate stamp.

2. SIMILES AND METAPHORS

Boldness and variety, which Virginia Woolf recommends to her young poet, are important characteristics of the mode of writing that seeks to work on emotions, i.e. her own quality of writing. Aristotle's *Poetics* and, especially, Longinus' *Peri Hupsous* could have been her manuals, for both Aristotle and Longinus had lifted up for special consideration the metaphor, the ambiguity of words, and the importance of rhythm with its perpetual beat, its opening and shutting. Aristotle, speaking of the excellence of diction in his *Poetics*, Chapter XXVI, recommends a mixture of »foreign, metaphorical, extended» words and common words. The former »will raise the language above the vulgar idiom, and common words will give it perspicuity».[1] As we saw in the previous chapter, this is in keeping with the vocabulary of *The Waves*. Further, both Aristotle and Longinus find a slight shock efficacious in bringing about poetic pleasure. Virginia Woolf practises what they teach: the reader is pushed and jolted into awareness by the shock-technique. Bold metaphors, unusual combinations and juxtapositions, together with the frequent use of antithesis are kept at hand as the principal means. In fact one finds

---

[1] Everyman's Library No. 901, p. 43.

the strategy to have been resorted to on the very title-page, where the author defiantly — we are reminded of Lily Briscoe — put: *'The Waves. A Novel.'*, and then proceeded to use every poetic device she could think of and as few novellistic ones as possible. *Lexis* and *taxis* are given the main attention; it is through them that *muthos*, *ethos*, and *dianoia* are to be revealed. Language is for Virginia Woolf above all a medium of symbolic expression. It is characteristic that it is 'the general force, a symbolic power'[1] that she specially praises in Aeschylus, Sophocles, and Euripides, whereas for instance C. M. Bowra's attention and admiration are primarily drawn to their hard thought.[2]

As *'The Waves. A Novel.'*, is in essence an extended metaphor, it is relevant that it should be propped from inside by the scaffolding of imagery. Longinus divides images into 'poetical' and 'oratorical', 'the former to astound, the latter to give perspicuity'[3]). I. A. Richards speaks of 'ornamental' and 'functional' respectively.[4] Virginia Woolf's images — the word used in its widest meaning — are often hard to classify, for 'ornamental' in her text also means 'functional'. Her language is related to the elaborate and suggestive quality of metaphysical poetry and to the romantic tradition, rather than to the 18th-century poetry, where the ornament is mostly employed expressly for adornment.[5] Poetical and functional qualities are combined in *The Waves*, for instance in the *thematic* imagery, such as the waves, willow, globe, carnation, and tree symbols employed structurally.[6] The same symbols are used in the role of *significant* images, i.e. to elucidate problems of reality, life, time, etc.[7] Colour-images are part of Virginia Woolf's impressionistic technique [8] serving both ornamental and functional purposes. Frequently, similes and metaphors in *The Waves* carry an excited, hyperbolical connotation, in keeping with the emphasis upon the intensity of creative experience and of the 'growing pains' of sensibility:

> I am like some vast sucker, some glutinous, some adhesive, some unsatiable mouth. (p. 143)

---

[1]) *On not Knowing Greek*, The Common Reader I, p. 49.
[2]) *Op. cit.*, p. 25.
[3]) *Op. cit.*, p. 294.
[4]) *Speculative Instruments*, p. 46.
[5]) Pope, with his subtlety and 'spider's touch', is a case apart.
[6]) Cf. the first chapter of this study.
[7]) Enlarged upon above in the second chapter.
[8]) See later pp. 57—63

I sit among you abrading your softness with my hardness, quenching the silver-grey flickering moth-wing quiver of words with the green spurt of my clear eyes. (p. 153)

The last metaphor contains several features that are typical of *The Waves*: unusual combinations, colour and other visual effects frequently combined with movement. Poetical, ornamental images are sometimes built out of very simple but effective materials:

... a moth-like impetuosity dashing itself against hard glass (p. 62)

Miss Matthews grumbles at my feather-headed carelessness. (p. 40)

I have been traversing the sunless territory of non-identity. (p. 8)

They have been crippled days, like moths with shrivelled wings unable to fly. (p. 38)

Life stands round me like glass round the imprisoned reed. (p. 137)

I flung words in fans like those the sower throws over the ploughed fields when the earth is bare. (p. 146)

At other times images are made up exclusively of matter-of-fact ingredients, which contribute to creating a very vividly descriptive picture:

There is the very powerful, bottle-green engine without a neck, all back and thighs, breathing steam. (p. 22)

The skirts of Miss Hudson and Miss Curry sweep by like candle extinguishers. (p. 16)

My heart turns rough; it abrades my side like a file with two edges. (p. 27)

I keep my phrases hung like clothes in a cupboard, waiting for someone to wear them. (p. 154)

I wish to free these bubbles from the trap-door in my head. (134)

The solemn and the commonplace need not fight shy of each other. Virginia Woolf follows the Johnsonian recommendation of a *discordia concors*: St. Paul's Cathedral is happily likened to

the brooding hen with spread wings from whose shelter run omnibuses and streams of men and women at the rush hour. (pp. 199—200)

Or, inside the cathedral

I stray and look and wonder, and sometimes, rather furtively, try to rise on the shaft of somebody else's prayer into the dome, out, beyond, wherever they go. But then like the lost and wailing dove, I find myself failing, fluttering, descending and perching upon some curious gargoyle, some battered nose or absurd tombstone, with humour, with wonder, and so again watch the sightseers with their Baedekers shuffling past, while the boy's voice soars in the dome and the organ now and then indulges in a moment of elephantine triumph. (p. 200)

Anti-climax is a favourite device with Virginia Woolf:

Let a man get up and say, 'Behold, this is the truth, and instantly I perceive a sandy cat filching a piece of fish in the background. (p. 133)

Abstract and concrete are mixed; big words recall trivial happenings.
The reader is now borne aloft, now abruptly brought down to earth.[1])
From one sentence to the next one never knows what kind of imagery
to expect. Imagery is thus made to reflect the incongruity and surprise
of life itself.[2]) Life, as Virginia Woolf sees it, is primarily composed of
confusion and fury:

> . . . great clouds always changing, and movement; something sulphurous
> and sinister, bowled up, helter-skelter; towering, trailing, broken off, lost,
> and I forgotten, minute, in a ditch. (p. 169)

Consequently images containing an element of movement and action
cover virtually any aspect of life, both in usual and unusual combinations:

> The world is beginning to move past me like the banks of a hedge when the
> train starts, like the waves of the sea when a steamer moves. (p. 134)
> . . . I rattle and bang through life, hitting first this side of the carriage, then
> the other . . (p. 58)
> But now silence falling pits my face, wastes my nose like a snowman, stood
> out in a yard in the rain. (p. 110)

An emotional experience, when conveyed through a sensuous image,
gains fullness and accuracy of representation. The mixing of abstract
and concrete elements contributes to giving deepened dimensions to
description:

> Exaltation, the doves descending, is over. (p. 110)
> Susan's agony shall be screwed tight into a ball. (p. 9)
> I will take my anguish and lay it upon the roots under the beech trees. (p. 9)
> I have a little dagger of contempt and severity hidden up my sleeve. (p. 154)
> It is as if one had woken in Stonehenge surrounded by a circle of great stones,
> these enemies, these presences. (p. 171)
> But some doubt remained. A shadow flitted through my mind like moths'
> wings among chairs and tables in a room in the evening. (p. 190)
> I had the intelligence to salute his integrity; his research with bony fingers

---

[1]) ROSEMOND TUVE calls the combination of widely discrepant elements 'a
radical image', used for swift lowering of the value or importance of something,
and quotes as an example T. S. Eliot's well-known 'I have measured out my life
with coffee spoons'. *Elisabethan and Metaphysical Imagery*, p. 130.

[2]) Cf. *Diary*, 28. 11. 28: » . . . I must include nonsense, fact, sordidity: but made
transparent. I think I must read Ibsen and Shakespeare and Racine.» (139) Virginia
Woolf may have had in mind King Lear who, at the height of a heart-rendingly
tragic scene produces a tremendous effect by his prosaic: »Pray you, undo this
button.» The feeling of the pitiableness of it all becomes doubly intense through
the anti-climax.

wrapped in rags because of chilblains for some diamond of indissoluble veracity. (p. 179)

... and then to be conscious of a ramrod of incorruptible sincerity ... (p. 180)

Typical of the two-level representation, a combination of abstract and concrete, the metaphysical and the physical, is the following extract, describing Bernard's mature contemplation towards the end of his life:

> The woods had vanished; the earth was a waste of shadow. No sound broke the silence of the wintry landscape. No cock crowed; no smoke rose; no train moved. A man without a self, I said. A heavy body leaning on a gate. A dead man. With dispassionate despair, with entire disillusionment, I surveyed the dust dance; my life, my friends, lives, and those fabulous presences, men with brooms, women writing, the willow tree by the river — clouds and phantoms made of dust too, of dust that changed, as clouds lose and gain and take gold or red and lose their summits and billow this way and that, mutable, vain. I, carrying a notebook, making phrases, had recorded mere changes; a shadow, I had been sedulous to take note of shadows. How can I proceed now, I said, without a self, weightless and visionless, through a world weightless, without illusion? (pp. 202−3)

The 'undifferentiated chaos of life', the stage at the beginning of the process towards maturity, is occasionally conveyed by synaesthesia and personification, suited for revealing the children's intensive, yet also still undifferentiated manner of perception:

> Now the cock crows like a spurt of hard, red water in the white tide. (p. 7)
> The yellow warmth in my side turned to stone ... (p. 10)
> Those are yellow words, those are fiery words, said Jinny. (p. 15)

Metonymic expressions, in the following sentences a hypallage, symbolize children's complete absorption in their perception of sensuous impressions:

> 'Those are white words', said Susan, 'like stones one picks up by seashore.' (p. 14)
> His rough and hairy voice is like an unshaven chin. (p. 26)
> ... the fly going buzz, buzz, buzz upon the nursery ceiling, and plates upon plates of innocent bread and butter. (p. 170)

Intensity makes nature a partaker in emotion: the corn sighs (p. 69), the fields sigh (p. 123), the leaves toss in agony (p. 179).

> The air no longer rolls its long, unhappy, purple waves over us. (p. 12)
> We were extinguished for a moment, went out like sparks in burnt paper and the blackness roared. (p. 197)

'As if' and 'like' are repeated on every page several times, for there is hardly a sentence without either a simile or a metaphor or both, or

even several of them. The interludes are composed out of them exclusively, with the simile slightly in predominance over the metaphor,
whereas in the text itself both appear with practically equal frequency.
Often a metaphor is strengthened by a tautological simile:

> ... the sea was slightly creased as if a cloth had wrinkles in it. (p. 5)

Mostly, however, the metaphor is invested with additional content by
the help of the simile:

> The waves drummed on the shore, like turbaned warriors, like turbaned men
> with poisoned assegais who, whirling their arms on high advance upon the
> feeding flocks, the white sheep. (p. 54)

Parallelism and heaping similes on top of metaphors add to the impression of profusion. Sense impressions, especially colour and light effects,[1])
make up most of the imagery in the interludes, naturally enough. On a
single page (e.g. p. 148), there may be as many as thirty-four of them.

The Waves is an account of 'a fanatical existence' (p. 79). The quality
of writing is made to conform to it through its tone of a mental and
emotional intoxication. Images are the links between the outer and the
inner worlds, the descriptive and the allegorical levels. »All metaphor
and simile», says John Middleton Murry,[2]) »can be described as the
analogy by which the human mind explores the universe of quality
and charts the non-measurable world». The 'non-measurable world' of
the artist's experience and achievement is in *The Waves* described
through, i.a., the following beautiful and successful cluster of images,
in many ways containing the gist of the whole novel:

> 'Like' and 'like' and 'like' — but what is the thing that lies beneath the sem-
> blance of the thing? Now that lightning has gashed the tree and the flowering
> branch has fallen and Percival, by his death, has made me this gift, let me
> see the thing. There is a square; there is an oblong. The players take the square
> and place it upon the oblong. They place it very accurately; they make a
> perfect dwelling-place. Very little is left outside. The structure is now visible;
> what is inchoate is here stated; we are not so various or so mean; we have
> made oblongs and stood them upon squares. This is our triumph; this is our
> consolation. (p. 116)

A really essential matter is conveyed with simple symbols and in short
sentences. The complicated, elaborate, and far-fetched analogies are
reserved for creating a Stimmung rather than for conveying a message
or elucidating something central in the author's vision.

---

[1]) Of which more in connection of impressionistic features, pp. 59—63
[2]) *Countries of the Mind*, p. 4.

3. INTENSIFYING FIGURES

The emotional excitement of *The Waves* is a typically romantic and a typically lyrical trait. The profusion of similes and metaphors, of questions and exclamations, of dashes and asides, of parallelisms and long rows of adjectives are all manifestations of the abandonment of reasoning in favour of the word-magic of an incantation. 'It is the speed, the hot, molten effect, the laval flow of sentence into sentence that I need', (p. 57) says Virginia Woolf's alter ego, Bernard. What she means by the 'laval flow of sentence' is, perhaps, illuminated through the following quotation:

> Here again there should be music. Not that wild hunting-song, Percival's music; but a painful, guttural, visceral, also soaring, lark-like, pealing song to replace these flagging, foolish transcripts — how much too deliberate! how much too reasonable! — which attempt to describe the flying moment of first love. (p. 177)

The Diary throws light upon the author's artistic intentions. While at work with *The Waves* she writes in her diary on January 7, 1931: »I want to make prose *move* — yes, I swear — as prose has never moved before, from the chuckle, the babble to rhapsody.»[1]) Her quality of a lyric poet becomes increasingly obvious the more one knows about her intentions.

The incantation-like quality of Virginia Woolf's writing becomes specially emphasized through what can be called the intensifying figures, hyperbole, climax, and repetition, which are such a marked characteristic of the style in *The Waves*. Through incantations the listener is, as it were, hypnotized by means of words and especially their rhythms to accept the singer's magical power over whatever he is trying to do, say, stopping bleeding. Virginia Woolf uses the same technique, letting rhythms penetrate to the subconscious level of the reader in order to give new meaningfulness to old manners of feeling, thinking and seeing, i.e. she works towards the purpose of poetry in making communication precede understanding.

John Crowe Ransom in his interesting article *Poetry as Primitive Language*[2]) divides language into conceptual (or rational) and imaginal

---

[1]) *Diary*, p. 165.
[2]) *The Writer and his Craft*, edited by Roy W. Cowden, Ann Arbor Books, The University of Michigan Press, 1954, p. 150.

(or substantival). »As a language develops», Ransom says, »and discourse becomes more rigorously conceptual, and the imaginal fringe of substance is obliterated from view, poetry intervenes. Poetry recovers to language its imaginal or substantival dimension, almost as fast as language loses it, though of course not quite. That is probably what poetry is for, as nearly as we can state it.»[1]) Virginia Woolf is trying to recover this lost quality of language in prose. She is looking for a medium which would combine the, to use a big word, holiness, the Logos-quality of words, with the current, sophisticated idiom of her own day and of her own circle. A certain primitiveness is to be allied to high civilization,[2]) which means that Virginia Woolf is trying to catch and apply the 'imaginal' quality of language which would penetrate all layers of the mind, not just the intellectual layer. Rhythm is of primary importance there. She replaces the metre of poetry by various rhythmical devices. The other special weapons of the poet, tropes and figures, are used by her with full force, some of them in downright reckless abundance.

A. HYPERBOLE

The use of hyperbole is not only a sign of excitement and of heightened sensibility, it is also a very feminine feature. *The Waves* is a thoroughly feminine book, with both the positive and negative connotations of the word. Virginia Woolf's feminism has aggressive features, which not only appear in *Three Guineas*, an intentionally propagandist book, but also in her novels. It is her strength as well as weakness, as she well knew herself. In *Mrs. Dalloway* and *To the Lighthouse* she succeeds in combining the woman's intuitive understanding of matters and the feminine quality of writing in a happy manner, but in *The Waves*, especially in the use of hyperbole, she becomes tempted into an irritating excess, irritating because hyperbole, used in such a degree, does not serve a purpose, as does, for instance, repetition.

The profusion of hyperbole can be handled best by subdividing the expressions into categories:

---

[1]) *Idem.*

[2]) cf. T. S. Eliot's statement (in a review on Wyndham Lewis's *Tarr* in The Egoist, Sept. 1918) about the artist being 'more primitive, as well as more civilized than his contemporaries', quoted by F. O. Matthiessen in *The Achievement of T. S. Eliot* (2nd ed.), p. 94. In *The Waves* this aspect becomes illustrated through recurrent image clusters, especially through Louis-imagery and the 'men with assegai'.

I. hyperbole expressed through numerical words like 'thousand', 'million',
and their multiples;

II. exaggerated expressions, made out of different categories of words;

III. hyperbolical imagery.

The dominant characteristics and themes of the novel are also reflected
through this device by its being connected with:

I. a. impressionist colour play

> Gradually the fibres of the burning bonfire were fused into one haze, one
> incandescence which lifted the weight of the woollen grey sky on top of it
> and turned it to a million atoms of soft blue. (p. 5)
> Jinny's eyes break into a thousand lights. (p. 11)

  b. time-space relations

> I seem already to have lived many thousand years. (pp. 48, 91, 119, 200)
> And the light of the stars falling, as it falls now, on my hand after travelling
> for millions upon millions of years — I could get a cold shock from that for
> a moment — not more, my imagination is too feeble. (p. 190)

  c. individual-mankind relations

> A million hands stitch, raise hods with bricks. (p. 125)
> Millions descend those stairs in a terrible descent ... Millions have died.
> (p. 137)
> But we — against the brick, against the branches, we six out of how many
> million millions, for one moment out of what measureless abundance of past
> time and time to come, burnt there triumphant. (p. 197)

  d. through antitheses creating depth-effects

> Far away on the horizon, among the million grains of blue-grey dust, burnt
> one pane, or stood the single line of one steeple or one tree. (p. 130)

II. Exaggerating adjectives include words pointing to numbers (myriad,[1])
innumerable, etc.), to size (huge, giant, gigantic, etc.), to time (primeval, infinite, etc.), or to intensified emotions (abysmal, tremendous, etc.). Substantives like 'giants' and 'mammoths', verbs like
'glare', 'devour', adverbs like 'immeasurably', 'infinitely', etc., also
add to the effect of emotional excitement:

  a. adjectives

> ... the incessant passage of traffic chafes us with distractions, and the door
> opening perpetually its glass cage solicits us with myriad temptations and
> offers insults and wounds to conscience ... (p. 88)

---

[1]) which, as CHRISTINE BROOKE-ROSE points out in her *Grammar of Metaphor*,
p. 4, combines hyperbole, synecdoche and metaphor.

To read this poem one must have myriad eyes, like one of those lamps that
turn on slabs of racing water at midnight in the Atlantic ... (p. 141)
The boy's voice soars in the dome and the organ now and then indulges in
a moment of elephantine triumph (p. 200)
my huge box (p. 21); a huge wheel (p. 25); the huge uproar (p. 52)
a monumental face (p. 24); monumental ladies (89)
the abysmal dullness of youth (p. 98)
the moment of ravenous identity (p. 102)
That is the flop of a giant toad in the undergrowth; that is the patter of some
primeval fir-cone falling to rot among the ferns. (p. 12)
... some gigantic amalgamation between the two discrepancies so hideously
apparent to me. (p. 38)

b. substantives

We are giants ... who can make forests quiver. (p. 16)
We have triumphed over the abysses of space, with rouge, with powder, with
flimsy pocket handkerchiefs. (p. 62)

c. verbs

the moon glared (p. 17); The blankness of the white table-cloth glares (p.
85); ... those painful silences, glaring as dry deserts, with every pebble
apparent; (p. 180)

d. involved in various devices:

Antithesis is here, as it is throughout the book, a favoured device:

... things are huge and very small (p. 16)
From the myriads of mankind and all time past he had chosen one person,
one moment in particular. (p. 194)

Tautology[1]), parallelism, and accumulation give additional weight to
emphasis:

For ever alone, alone, alone (p. 159); the long, long history (p. 48)
That is Percival, lounging on the cushions, monolithic, in giant repose. (p. 59)
I am astonished, as I draw the veil off things with words, how much, how
infinitely more than I can say, I have observed. (p. 61)

III. Hyperbolical images contribute to stretching the vistas further in time and space:

Leaves are as high as the domes of vast cathedrals (p. 16)
Now open in my eyes a thousand eyes of curiosity. (p. 103)
I cannot move without dislodging the weight of centuries. (p. 76)
I shall be blown down the eternal corridors for ever. (p. 113)

---

[1]) The rhetorical devices and expressions used are in accordance with the
definitions in OLAF HOMÉN's *Poetik*, pp. 203 ff. Tautology does not here carry
a pejorative connotation.

B. Climax

Climax is comparatively rare, often to be considered an accumulation rather than a genuine climax.

> I see wild birds, and impulses wilder than the wildest birds strike my wild heart. My eyes are wild. (p. 42)
> I who had been thinking myself so vast, a temple, a church, a whole universe . . . (p. 207)

An accruing effect has in the following chain of sentences been brought about by enlarging the original phrase:

> What forces, he asks, staring at the gas-fire with his shoulders hunched up more hugely than we know them (he is in his shirt-sleeves remember), have brought me to this? What vast forces? he thinks, getting into the stride of his majestic phrases as he looks over his shoulder at the window. . . . What vast forces of good and evil have brought me here? he asks . . . (p. 136)

C. Repetition

This is by far the most frequent figure in *The Waves*, appearing in all its varieties and nuances, interconnected with other figures within its own sphere and drawing in others. It serves to form rhythm, to heighten the intensity (one is reminded of Macbeth's 'to-morrow, and to-morrow, and to-morrow'), to prop up the structure through the recurrent leit-motifs and image clusters. It emphasizes the wave-like movement, heightens the feeling of insecurity and transitoriness of human life, the smallness and helplessness of a human being. Occasionally it may convey a suggestively terrifying effect.

Verbs, substantives, adjectives, adverbs, pronouns, and longer clauses appear in large numbers in all the different groups of this figure:

I. repetition of a word (*tautology* or *pleonasm*)

   1. with a connective

   a. verbs

> A great beast's foot is chained. It stamps and stamps and stamps on the shore (pp. 6, 42, 49)
> . . . this great clock, yellow-faced, which ticks and ticks (p. 14)
> Let me cast and throw away this veil of being, this cloud that changes with the least breath, night and day, and all night and all day. (p. 209)

   b. substantives

> Words and words and words, how they gallop . . . (p. 59)
> I like the passing of face and face and face, deformed, indifferent. (p. 114)
> Faces recur, faces and faces . . . (p. 182)

Then suddenly, in a moment of exasperation, off to Cumberland with a quiet man for a whole week in an inn, with the rain running down the window-panes and nothing but mutton and mutton and again mutton for dinner. (p. 182)

... the appetite for happiness and happiness, and still more happiness is glutted. (p. 103)

c. adjectives and adverbs

... the birds ... now sang in chorus, shrill and sharp (p. 53). (pleonasm and alliteration)

quicker and quicker (p. 7); faster and faster (p. 9);

You have gone across the court, further and further, drawing finer and finer the thread between us. (p. 110)

'Like' and 'like' and 'like' — but what is the thing that lies beneath the semblance of the thing? (p. 116)

But she is blind after the light and trips and flings herself down on the roots under the trees, where the light seems to pant in and out, in and out. (p. 10)

d. pronouns

I shall let them wall me away from you, from you and from you (p. 28)

... I sign my name, I, and again I, and again I. (pp. 118, 121)

2. without a connective (*epizeuxis*), often connected with exclamation and onomatopoeia:[1])

... the fly going buzz, buzz, buzz, upon the nursery ceiling ... (p. 170)

Louis! Louis! Louis! they shout. (p. 8)

Sleep, sleep, I croon. Sleep, I sing. Sleep, sleep, sleep, I say. (p. 122)

I, I, I, tired as I am, spent as I am ... (p. 210)

I rose and walked away — I, I, I; (p. 180)

Nothing, nothing, nothing broke with its fin that leaden waste of waters. (p. 174)

Out rush a bristle of horned suspicions, horror, horror, horror — (p. 178)

»That is the first stroke of the church bell», said Louis. »Then the others follow; one, two; one, two; one, two.» (p. 8)

We have sacrificed the embrace among the ferns, and love, love, love by the lake, standing, like conspirators who have drawn apart to share some secret, by the urn. (p. 164)

II. a word or expression at the beginning and at the end of a sentence (*epanalempsis*)

I have signed my name ... already twenty times, I, and again I, and again I. (p. 118)

Sleep, I say, sleep. (p. 122)

---

[1]) For further examples see sound-impressions, pp. 63—65

III. repetition in a reverse order (*epanodos*):

The camel is a vulture; the vulture a camel. (p. 27)

Motor-cars, vans, motor-omnibuses, and again motor-omnibuses, vans, motor-cars — they pass the window. (p. 67)

»It is hate, it is love», said Susan — —. »It is love», said Jinny, »it is hate». (p. 98)

Opening and shutting, shutting and opening, with increasing hum and sturdiness, the haste and fever of youth are drawn into service until the whole being seems to expand in and out like the mainspring of a clock. (p. 183)

IV. repetition of the last word of a sentence at the beginning of the next (*anadiplosis*): [1])

We shall meet to-night, thank Heaven. Thank Heaven, I need not be alone. (p. 83)

To be contracted by another person into a single being — how strange. How strange to feel the line that is spun from us lengthening its fine filament across the misty spaces of the intervening world. (p. 64)

The being grows rings, like a tree. Like a tree, leaves fall. (p. 201)

In the following passage repetition, with *anadiplosis* included, produces a corrosive effect:

And time . . . lets fall its drop. The drop that has formed on the roof of the soul falls. On the roof of my mind time, forming lets fall its drop. Last week, as I stood shaving, the drop fell. (p. 131)

V. varied repetitive arrangements within a longer passage:

Now there is this gulping ceremony with my mother, this handshaking ceremony with my father; now I must go on waving, I must go on waving, till we turn the corner. Now that ceremony is over. Heaven be praised, all ceremonies are over. I am alone; I am going to school for the first time. Everybody seems to be doing things for this moment only; and never again. Never again. The urgency of it all is fearful. Everybody knows I am going to school, going to school for the first time. 'That boy is going to school for the first time', says the housemaid, cleaning the steps. (p. 21)

The repetitive devices are important in contributing effectively to the impression of a billowing movement, linking the fragmentary with the continuous.

D. PARALLELISM, ACCUMULATION, AND AMPLIFICATION

The three of them are closely connected, being variations of the same theme, as it were: parallelism includes several expressions for one thing,

---

[1]) *Epanodos* and *anadiplosis* contain an antithetical element, reminding one of *chiasmus*, though without an inversion.

accumulation is characterized by a rich use of adjectives and substantives, amplification develops the given theme further and uses other figures, exclamation, rhetorical question, apostrophe, simile, etc., in building up the construction. »The author», says Longinus on amplification, »brings on one impressive point after another in a continuous and ascending scale».[1]) Virginia Woolf uses parallelism without connectives (*asyndeton*) rather than with them (*polysyndeton*)[2]). Repetitions of words at the beginning (*anaphora*) or at the end (*epiphora*) of a sentence are fairly regularly connected with it.

I. *parallelism*

a. with anaphora and asyndeton, intensity becoming increased:

We all rise; we all stand up. (p. 18)
I sink, I fall; — But they stretch; they elongate. (p. 20)
My eyes swell; my eyes prick with tears. (p. 23)
... he ... is writing in such an off-hand, such a slap-dash way ... (p. 56)
That is the mean; that is the average. (p. 67)
This is the truth. This is the fact. (pp. 107—8)
Hence our loneliness; hence our desolation. (p. 111)
What is startling, what is unexpected, what we cannot account for, what turns symmetry to nonsense — that comes suddenly to my mind, thinking of him. (p. 172)

b. with epiphora and asyndeton

... the grey cloth became barred with thick strokes moving, one after another, beneath the surface, following each other, pursuing each other, perpetually. (p. 5)
the immitigable tree, the implacable tree (p. 17)

c. with anaphora and epiphora

If that blue could stay for ever; if that hole could could remain for ever; if this moment could stay for ever — —. (p. 27)

II. *accumulation*, giving an impression of a searching and analytic mind:

... let us begin this new chapter, and observe the formations of this new, this unknown, strange, altogether unidentified and terrifying experience — the new drop — which is about to shape itself. (p. 135)

---

[1]) *Op. cit.*, p. 289.
[2]) This is a reflection of the 'atomistic' vision of the author and of her laying stress on the fragmentary rather than the continuous in the depiction. Continuity, again, is implied in the stream- of- consciousness method and in the general pattern of the novel.

> Unhappy, unfriended, in exile he would sometimes, in moments of confidence, describe how the surf swept over the beaches of his home. (p. 173)
>
> I hear tramplings, tremblings, stirrings round me. (p. 8)

III. *amplification*

> I grasp, I hold fast, said Susan, I hold firmly to his hand, anyone's with love, with hatred; it does not matter which. (p. 162)
>
> I mount; I escape; I rise on spring-heeled boots over the tree-tops. (p. 20)

It is customary in *The Waves* to have several figures combined in a passage. The following extract, in many ways typical impressionism, contains *symploke* (anaphora and epiphora used in a sentence group), *circle* (a passage starting and finishing off with the same expression or word), *asyndeton, polysyndeton*, and *inversion*:

> Mine is the heron that stretches its vast wings lazily; and the cow that creaks as it pushes one foot before another munching; and the wild, swooping swallow; and the faint red in the sky; and the green when the red fades; the silence and the bell; the call of the man fetching cart-horses from the fields — all are mine. (p. 70)

The intensifying figures, repetition above all, serve an important structural purpose in *The Waves*. While words may in their prolific abundance remind the reader of water spurting from a fountain, under great pressure, the structure of sentences corresponds to the shaping element. Rhythm has a doubly important role in *The Waves*, the flux of life and the stream of consciousness being both subjected to its movement. Especially repetition, in all its variations, seems indispensable. Its suggestiveness contributes in particular both to symbolism and rhythm.

> It is the effort and the struggle, it is the perpetual warfare, it is the shattering and piecing together — this is the daily battle, defeat or victory, the absorbing pursuit. The trees, scattered, put on order; the thick green of the leaves thinned itself to a dancing light. I netted them under with a sudden phrase. I retrieved them from formlessness with words. (p. 191)

4. IMPRESSIONISM, EXPRESSIONISM AND SYMBOLISM

Virginia Woolf's technique in *The Waves* is an amalgamation of impressionistic and expressionistic devices. Eva Weidner in her study[1] finds the latter more strongly represented in *The Waves* than in any

---

[1] *Impressionismus und Expressionismus in den Romanen Virginia Woolfs*, p. 112

other novel by Virginia Woolf. I find impressionism employed predominantly in the elaborate details of representation, while expressionism is more a matter of larger patterns and general attitudes. The mixture of the two techniques corresponds to the two-way direction of the author's vision, to her intention to find a unifying link between the passing and the permanent. She finds something of it reflected in the stream of consciousness, which retains the perceived, as it were, in an ever-present *now*. She moves in her representation from the phenomena into the perceiving consciousness as well as from the consciousness towards phenomena. Impressionistic devices help to create the 'now', the vanishing moment, the chaotic detail; expressionistic devices, such as the allegorical representation and the typified characters, imply the semblance of permanence, the existence of order, pointing to Platonic 'ideas'.

IMPRESSIONISTIC FEATURES

I shall start this section by quoting and analyzing a short extract, which will serve as an introduction to further examination of the novel in this light.

How then does light return to the world after the eclipse of the sun? Miraculously. Frailly. In thin stripes. I hangs like a glass cage. It is a hoop to be fractured by a tiny jar. There is a spark there. Next moment a flush of dun. Then a vapour as if earth were breathing in and out, once, twice, for the first time. Then under the dullness someone walks with a green light. Then off twists a white wraith. The woods throb blue and green, and gradually the fields drink in red, gold, brown. Suddenly a river snatches a blue light. The earth absorbs colour like a sponge slowly drinking water. It puts on weight; rounds itself; hangs pendent; settles and swings beneath our feet. (p. 203)

Analysis discloses in it the following traits characteristic of impressionistic writing:

In *vocabulary*, colours are the first to draw attention. Blue and green are mentioned twice, red, gold, brown, dun, white once. Visual effects are also conveyed through substantives (light, eclipse, sun, glass, spark, flush, dullness, wraith, vapour, colour). Further word-painting is done by the help of verbal imagery. The verbs of the last sentence contain a visual aspect combined with action and movement, embodying the basic descriptive elements in *The Waves*. The adverbs, forming one-word sentences, are here an illuminating example of 'pointillism' in word-painting.

Considering *syntactical* aspects, parataxis with asyndeton is used throughout the passage. The last sentence is a typical example of Virginia Woolf's use of the semicolon to emphasize the abruptness, fragmentariness of phenomena, their splash-like character. Substantives predominate; the adverbial construction is accentuated by being given a detached position.

Of syntactical irregularities, ellipsis and inversion are used, the former as many as five times within this short extract, the latter once. Of *figures* of speech, question and a hyperbolic element (miraculously, tiny) appear. Three similes, with both 'as if' and 'like', as well as several metaphors are included. In fact, nearly all of the sentences contain some kind of metaphoric statement. 'The fields drink', 'a river snatches', 'the woods throb blue and green' are examples of animism.

The analysis of the elements of rhythm shows that parallelism, both in the arrangement of sentences and in that of words, plays an important role. Repetition with anaphora (three consecutive sentences beginning with 'then') gives the sentences a swinging movement, with accumulation ('breathing in and out, once, twice, for the first time'), antithesis ('in and out', 'the spark — a dun'), and the ing-forms contributing their share to the billowing of the rhythm. The formula, here in miniature, is repeated throughout the novel in smaller and larger patterns.

I. VOCABULARY

A. WORD-PAINTING

a. Visual impressions

The first thing that strikes the reader throughout the novel is the wealth of colour, light, and other visual images. Especial use has been made of them in the nature descriptions, twelve pages in all, which are inserted to create the background in which the permanent phenomenon, the sun's journey, is combined with the instantaneous and changing happenings of the 'now'. (In the allegorical pattern the interludes represent moments of heightened emotional states.) These twelve pages alone contain as many as 161 different colour effects, 131 of them pure colours, 23 connected with light (pale, dark, bright, light, etc.), and 7 verbal forms (blacken, brown, darken, colour, redden, purple, whiten). Images connected with visual effects are innumerable. Some idea of their wealth is perhaps given by the fact that there are 31 on the first page alone. The scenery is made to swim in the light, in the impressionistic painter's manner, with the background remaining hazy, while the foreground steps forward from the canvas:

> Far away on the horizon, among the million grains of blue-grey dust, burnt one pane, or stood the single line of one steeple or one tree. The red curtains and the white blinds blew in and out, flapping against the edge of the window, and the light which entered by flaps and breadths unequally had in it some brown tinge, and some abandonment as it blew through the blowing curtains in gusts. Here it browned a cabinet, there reddened a chair, here it made the window waver in the side of the green jar. (p. 130)

Bright colours are at first predominant, the process starting from the sunrise,

> as if the arms of a woman couched beneath the horizon had raised a lamp . . . (p. 5),

proceeding into a full blaze of colours:

> . . . for now at midday the garden was all blossom and profusion and even the tunnels under the plants were green and purple and tawny as the sun beat through the red petal, or the broad yellow petal, or was barred by some thickly furred green stalk. (p. 107)

With the sun's journey across the sky over, the nuances change into darker shades:

> Black and grey were shot into the garden from the broken vessel that had once held red light. (p. 167)

The story-sections of the novel contain some 800 colour and light images, often several appearing within a single sentence. *White*, popular with the impressionists, appears 75 times, alone and in various combinations (moon-white, pearl-white; white-domed, -haired, -ruffed, -tented; whiten; whiteness). Mushrooms are white-domed, foam is a white of pearl on the misty sand, pastures are moon-white, a serpent, curled crimson, has white scales, butterflies are 'red admirals and cabbage whites'; an elephant is white with maggots, a dead man's jowl is white as a dead codfish, to mention a few rather unusual examples.

red appears in 23 shades and combinations (amethystine, fiery, foxy, fulvous, pink, plum, purple, puce, red-brown, reddish, rose, vinous; red-edged, red-hot; cherry, fire, poppy, strawberry, wine; faint, filmed, flaming, mottled red).

blue (aquamarine, blue-green, blue-grey, grey-blue, lilac, violet, deep-, pale-, soft-, steel-blue).

grey (blue-grey, grey-blue, pearl-grey, silver; ash-, clay-, dun-, moth-, slate-, stone-coloured).

green (blue-green, bottle-green, emerald, grass-green, green-sea, sea-green, green-veined, yellowish green).

yellow (canary, flaxen, fulvous, gilt, gold(en), orange, tawny, topaz, umber; yellow-faced, -glazed, -plated).

Brown and *black* are, as is natural, much rarer colours, employed mainly to describe the scenery after sunset (pp. 167-8).

Epithets like ambiguous (draperies), chocolate-brown, coffee-coloured, diamond-tipped, incandescent, lemon-coloured, moonlight-coloured, moonlit, nacreous, opalescent, opaque (dress), pallid, phosphorescent, resplendent, storm-tinted, sun-spotted, translucent, water-coloured, water-globed (jewels), etc., add to the colour-play.

Compound epithets with the second participle ending in *-ed* are an impressionistic feature.[1] There are 55 different compounds of that type, used 86 times. Sixteen of them end with *-coloured*, 39 with other verbs, in 13 of them the first part being connected with some colour. Sometimes they are lavishly massed together within a single sentence:

> There is a red carnation in that vase. A single flower as we sat there waiting, but now a seven-sided flower, many-petalled, red, puce, purple-shaded, stiff with silver-tinted leaves — a whole flower to which every eye brings its contribution. (p. 91)[2]

Substantives denoting visual impressions cover a wide range, as is natural. 'Light' appears on most pages several times, often connected

---

[1] Cf. WEIDNER, *op.cit.*, p. 28, and AATOS OJALA, *Aestheticism and Oscar Wilde*, Part II, Literary Style, pp. 163ff. For my information on impressionism I have also drawn on LUISE THON's *Die Sprache des deutschen Impressionismus* and ELISE RICHTER's *Impressionismus, Expressionismus und Grammatik*, in Zeitschrift für Romanische Philologie, XLVII Band 1929, pp. 349—71; STEPHEN ULLMANN, *Style in the French Novel*, MARTIN TURNELL, *The Art of French Fiction*, MARGIT ABENIUS, *Stilstudier i Kellgrens prosa;* HELGE GULLBERG, *Berättarkonst och stil i Per Hallströms prosa*, JARL LOUHIJA, *Symbolit ja kielikuvat Bertel Gribenbergin tuotannossa* and LEEVI VALKAMA, *Tutkimus Johannes Linnankosken 'Pakolaisten' tyylistä*.

[2] A famous point of comparison is KEATS' *The Eve of St. Agnes*, in which he has 54 epithets ending in -ed. He far outdoes Virginia Woolf with his 'poppied warmth of sleep', 'azure-lidded sleep', 'woofed phantasies', 'sole-thoughted', 'be-nightmared', and other original formations.

with imagery denoting quick movement, such as that of arrows, daggers, darting spears:

> Red and gold shot through the waves, in rapid running arrows, feathered with darkness. (p. 147)

> Then another cloud was caught in the light and another and another, so that the waves beneath were arrow-struck with fiery feathered darts that shot erratically across the quivering blue. (p. 117)

Shades of light are conveyed through words like blackness, blaze, clarity, darkness (on p. 168 as many as seven times on eleven lines), dimness, dullness, gleam, glare, haze, incandescence, shadow, shine, tinge, tint, transparency, etc. Besides the natural sources of light, the sun and the moon, artefacts like candelabra, candle, cresset, lamp, lighthouse, torch are employed, as well as other man-made and natural sources, or parts of sources of light: bonfire, conflagration, fire(light), flame, glow-worm, ray, spark, taper.

Verbs connected with light contribute to creating the effect of instantaneous, detached, vanishing phenomenon (flare, flash, flicker. glitter, twinkle), or they give the feeling of intensity (blaze, glare, flare, gleam), or help to create Stimmung (darken, fade, shadow, shade, shine),

> Erratically rays of light flashed and wandered, like signals from sunken islands, or darts shot through laurel groves by shameless, laughing boys. (p. 147)

> And burning lights from the window-panes flash in and out on the grasses . . . (p.7)

> . . . and then the lights of London — not the flaring ecstasy of youth, not the tattered violet banner, but still the light of London all the same; hard, electric lights, high up in offices; street lamps laced along dry pavements, flares roaring above street markets. (p. 192)

> The sun struck straight upon the house, making the white walls glare between the dark windows. (p. 107)

> How humiliating never to be sure what to say next, and those painful silences, glaring as dry deserts, with every pebble apparent; (p. 180)

> The height from floor to ceiling was hung with vast curtains of shaking darkness. The looking-glass was pale as the mouth of a cave shadowed by hanging creepers. (p. 168)

Adverbs are not often employed in light imagery. In general their task in *The Waves* is to create rhythms and cadences rather than give pointillistic light effects. Occasionally, as shown above[1]), they are very effectively used for that purpose. Examples of rhythmical arrangements:

> But Neville, delicately avoiding interference, stealthily, like a conspirator, hastens back to his room. (p. 65)

---

[1]) cf. p. 58

And then tiring of pursuit and flight, lovelily they came descending, delicately declining, dropped down and sat silent in the tree ... (p. 53)

A few of the light images strike the reader as being somewhat cliché-like. So, for instance:

I sink down on the black plumes of sleep; its thick wings are pressed to my eyes. (p. 20)

The swallow dips her wings; the moon rides through the blue seas alone. (p. 76)

We have no more to expose ourselves on the bare hedges to the wind and snow; ... or stay, unmurmuring, on those pallid noondays when the bird creeps close to the bough ... and the damp whitens the leaf. (p. 199)[1])

The purple light in Miss Lambert's ring passes to and fro across the black stain on the white page of the Prayer Book. It is vinous, it is an amorous light. (p. 24)

The last image is enlarged upon later in the novel, now in a graphic manner, connected with original imagery:

And Miss Lambert, Miss Cutting and Miss Bard, ... monumental ladies, white-ruffed, stone-coloured, enigmatic, with amethyst rings moving like virginal tapers, dim glow-worms over the pages of French, geography and arithmetic, presided ... (p. 89)

Colour and light imagery is applied to every kind of object: silences glare, ecstasy flares, 'my being only glitters when all its facets are exposed to many people' (p. 132). Throughout the book word-painting serves the purpose of intensification of emotion and Stimmung, involving all the senses.

b. O t h e r   s e n s e   i m p r e s s i o n s: s o u n d,   s m e l l,   t a s t e, t o u c h

Nature descriptions are employed to convey intense emotional states when all the senses are on the alert. 'Chaotic enumeration'[2]) is a device well suited for giving an impression of intoxication:

You know that sudden rush of wings, that exclamation, carol and confusion; the riot and babble of voices; and all the drops are sparkling, trembling, as if the garden were a splintered mosaic, vanishing, twinkling; not yet formed into one whole; and a bird sings close to the window. (p. 175)

---

[1]) 'Pallid' was favoured by the romantics: Wordsworth uses it fifteen times, Poe has 'a pallid bust of Pallas' in *The Raven*, Keats, 'pallid' moonshine' in *The Eve of St.Agnes*.

[2]) The term is Leo Spitzer's; cf. *Linguistics and Literary History*, p. 206.

Sound images are not quite as ubiquitous as visual, but they are a good second in the group of expressions for sensuous approach. Onomatopoeia plays an important role, often connected with tautology.[1]

> I snatched the telephone and the buzz, buzz, buzz of its stupid voice . . . battered my heart down. (p. 127)
>
> the fly going buzz, buzz, buzz . . . (p. 170)
>
> Cheep, cheep creaks the fire, like the cheep of insects . . . (p. 142)
>
> Jug, jug, jug, I sing like the nightingale. (p. 126)
>
> Knock, knock, knock. Must, must, must. Must go, must sleep, must wake, must get up — (p. 166)
>
> . . . the tap, tap, tap of the remorseless youth. (p. 205)
>
> Silence falls; silence falls; . . . But now listen; tick, tick; hoot, hoot; the world has hailed us back to it. (p. 160)

Sound effects get reinforcement through vowels and consonants: trees and waves murmur, London hums and murmurs, the door creaks, the blood gurgles down the gutter, flesh is gashed, steamers thud, the savage beast stamps, birds carry bits of straw bubbling and chuckling, a boy's voice wails round the dome like some lost and wandering dove, the wind washes through the elm trees.

Alliteration is frequently connected with sound images:

> In the garden the birds . . . now sang together in chorus, shrill and sharp; (p. 53)

'Roar' is a frequently employed intensifying image: not only trains, trams, omnibuses, waters, flares but also silence, blackness and the pageant of existence roar.

> The sound of the chorus came across the water and I felt leap up that old impulse, which has moved me all my life, to be thrown up and down on the roar of other people's voices, singing the same song; to be tossed up and down on the roar of almost senseless merriment, sentiment, triumph, desire. (p. 198)

There is an element of synaesthesia in the previous example. The following is an obvious case of *l'audition colorée*, coloured hearing:

> All separate sounds — wheels, bells, the cries of drunkards, of merrymakers — are churned into one sound, steel blue, circular. (p. 97)

The characters are connected with different smells, Susan with country smells: of pine, or of the cold green air, Rhoda, with violets. Rhoda's disgust of human beings en masse is expressed through the

---

[1] cf. above, p. 54

smells of sweat and of cheap scent. School is connected with the carbolic smell of corridors and the chalky smell of schoolrooms. Smells of decay and rottenness are frequently implied in imagery.[1]) Virginia Woolf does not use smell as a thematic device in the same way as for instance Proust or Faulkner, whose honeysuckle in *The Sound and the Fury* inevitably recalls Proust's hawthorne and madeleine.

Taste does not play a great role in *The Waves*, but there is a graphic passage describing 'delicious mouthfuls of roast duck' proceeding 'past my palate, down my gullet, into my stomach' accompanied by

cool wine, fitting glove-like over those finer nerves that seem to tremble from the roof of my mouth and make it spread (as I drink) into a domed cavern, green with vine leaves, musk-scented, purple with grapes. (p. 99)

A mixture of sensations appears in the following image:

I ... feel her laughter curl its tongues of fire round me ... (p. 87)

Touch and sound are mixed in one example of hypallage:

His rough and hairy voice is like an unshaven chin. (p. 26)

It is typical of impressionism to detach the attribute from its object, to let, as it were, the senses rush towards their object of perception tumbling on top of each other. In the previous example touch beats sound in the race. A touch-sensation, cold water running along the spine, is included in the recurrent images. (pp. 19, 170, 205)

B. EPITHETS

The expansion of vocabulary, characteristic of impressionistic writing, makes itself specially felt in the use of the epithet. As seen in earlier contexts of this study, an abundance of attributes is one of the dominant features in *The Waves*, naturally enough, as the emphasis upon the epithet is yet another means to create a pictorial effect. Heaping epithets on top of each other also helps to create a reflection of the tentative, fumbling manner of a mental process:

Not that wild hunting-song, Percival's music; but a painful, guttural, visceral, also soaring, lark-like pealing song to replace these flagging, foolish transcripts — (p. 177)

---

[1]) Rotten apples, mentioned several times (pp. 12, 54, 167) are reminiscent of Schiller who liked to have them in his desk and found their smell helpful for artistic creation; cf. PRESS, *op. cit.*, p. 78; Sibelius, it is said, found the smell of soaked flax stimulating.

> Let me denounce this piffling, trifling, self-satisfied world, these horse-hair seats, these coloured photographs of piers and parades. (p. 51)

Synonyms, or near-synonyms, are used in great numbers, in keeping with the general evocative tone:

> I was Byron, and the tree was Byron's tree, lachrymose, down-showering, lamenting. (p. 60)
>
> At that hour your relationship is mute, null, dun-coloured. (p. 151)
>
> I am like some vast sucker, some glutinous, some adhesive, some insatiable mouth. (p. 143)

The tendency towards brevity and an instantaneous effect of expression, 'an immediate synthesis', is also reflected in this connection through a special form of contraction, the use of the substantive for the adjective:[1]

> ... and then the mystic sense of completion and then that rasping, dog-fish skin-like roughness — (p. 178)
>
> ... the moth-wing quiver of words. (p. 153)

A misapplication of a word (*hypallage*) greatly adds to the force of the image, as seen in the examples in *The Waves:*

> His rough and hairy voice is like an unshaven chin. (p. 26)
>
> ... the fly going buzz, buzz, buzz upon the nursery ceiling and plates upon plates of innocent bread and butter. (p. 170)

L'épithète rare is a special feature of *l'écriture artiste*, of which *The Waves* is the most prominent illustration in the English language since the symbolist fashion at the turn of the century. But there is a greater concreteness in Virginia Woolf's use of the epithet than there is, say, in Wilde's, with less affectation and far-fetched floweriness, often forming what Warren and Wellek call 'radical images'.[2]

> ... down in the valley the train draws across the fields lop-eared with smoke. (p. 204)
>
> ... the last drop ... that we let fall like some supernal quicksilver into the swelling and splendid moment created by us from Percival. (p. 104)
>
> ... in a moment of elephantine triumph. (p. 200)
>
> ... all the blades of the grass were run together in one fluent green blaze. (p. 106)

---

[1] on this device cf., e.g. L. SPITZER, *Stilstudien* I, pp. 6—8, and A. OJALA, *op. cit.*, p. 30

[2] AUSTIN WARREN & RENÉ WELLEK, *The Theory of Literature*, p. 208; also cf. ROSEMOND TUVE, *op. cit.*, p. 130.

In impressionism, as Ojala points out[1]), the mode of apperception is based on 'spatial' relations, in symbolism the key-word is 'temporal'. The space-time relations are in impressionism embedded in syntactical arrangements with a special abundance of variety.

II. SYNTAX

A. SENTENCE STRUCTURE

a. General

The combination of simple structures and long, rambling sentences that characterizes *The Waves* is yet another device to illustrate the mental processes and to create the illusion of something at the same time spontaneous, abrupt, yet flux-like.

> Life comes; life goes; we make life. So you say. (p. 125)

> Here is the ticket collector. Here are two men; three women; there is a cat in a basket; myself with my elbow on the window-sill — this is here and now. (p. 47)

The dominant structure is, surprisingly, considering the elaborate stamp of the writing in *The Waves*, the asyndetic parataxis, i.e. main clauses without connectives, but the author manages to invest it with great variety through inserted syntactical and rhetorical devices:

> I am for ever sleeping and waking. Now I sleep; now I wake. I see the gleaming tea-urn; the glass cases full of pale-yellow sandwiches; the men in round coats perched on stools at the counter; and also behind them, eternity. (p. 69)

Occasionally polysyndeton and hypotaxis are employed in an exaggerated manner to add to the impression of casualness and close-to-consciousness feeling:

> What the dead poet said, you have forgotten. And I cannot translate it to you so that its binding power ropes you in, and makes it clear to you that you are aimless; and the rhythm is cheap and worthless; and so remove that degradation which, if you are unaware of your aimlessness, pervades you, making you senile, even while you are young. (p. 68)

Polysyndeton is employed especially when the speaker allows his thought to float freely in the stream of consciousness:

> The little apparatus of observation is unhinged. Pillars go down; the Doctor floats off; some sudden exaltation possesses me. He was thrown, riding in a

---

[1]) *op. cit.*, p. 31

race, and when I came along Shaftesburg Avenue to-night, those insignificant
and scarcely formulated faces that bubble up out of the doors of the Tube,
and many obsure Indians, and people dying of famine and disease, and women
who have been cheated, and whipped dogs and crying children — all these
seemed to me bereft. (p. 172)

The reader is allowed to follow the very action of the mental process,
with its free-associational fluctuation. Ellipsis, polysyndeton, sentence
parallelism, the detached expression at the end of the sentence, all
contribute towards that purpose. The ubiquitous semicolon works to
the same end, giving the expression a semblance of fragmentariness
and breathlessness[1].) It also serves to separate the effect from its cause,
thus emphasizing the impressionistic juxtaposition of phenomena, often
in antithetical combinations:

What a litter — what a confusion; with here birth, here death; succulence
and sweetness; effort and anguish; and myself always running hither and
thither. (p. 202)

An outstanding example of the use of the semicolon may serve as an
illustration of Virginia Woolf's idiosyncratic punctuation in general:

Susan, I respect; because she sits stitching. (p. 69)

b. N o m i n a l   c o n s t r u c t i o n s

Impressionism favours the substantives, expressionism the verbs.
Both tendencies are to be seen in *The Waves*, with the nominal forms
predominating. Examples of them can be found on nearly every page.

I caught my train. An so back to London in the evening. How satisfactory,
the atmosphere of common sense and tobacco; old women clambering into
their third-class carriage with their baskets; the sucking at pipes; the good-
nights and see you tomorrows of friends parting at wayside stations, and
then the lights of London — not the flaring ecstasy of youth, not that tat-
tered violet banner, but still the light of London all the same; street lamps
laced along dry pavements; flares roaring above street markets. (pp. 191—2)

Sometimes a sentence is reduced to one word, with emphasis
falling heavily on it. Martin Turnell rightly calls attention to the
'lapidary' quality of a verbless sentence.[2])
This device, like the placing of the free adjunct, is above all connected
with rhythm and with the illustration of a gliding movement towards

---

[1]) Virginia Woolf's interest in Sir Thomas Browne and De Quincey may have
had an influence on her use of semicolons.

[2]) *op. cit.*, p. 24

an important stop, where the crucial expression or word is sure to catch attention.

> But you exist somewhere. Something of you remains. A judge. (p. 110)
> The old woman pauses against the lit window. A contrast. (p. 66)
> What do we feel on meeting? Sorrow. (p. 150)
> Let up stop for a moment; let us behold what we have made. Let it blaze against the yew trees. One life. There. It is over. Gone out. (p. 62)
> How richly I shall enjoy my youth (you make me feel). And London. And freedom. But stop. (p. 61)

Virginia Woolf employs the verbless structure also to reproduce the stream of consciousness:

> So into the street again, swinging my stick, looking at wire trays in stationers shop-windows, at baskets of fruit grown in the colonies, murmuring Pillicock sat on Pillicock's hill, or Hark, hark, the dogs do bark, or The World's great age begins anew, or Come away, come away, death — mingling nonsense and poetry, floating in the stream. (p. 200)

The immediacy becomes greatly heightened through the avoidance of verbs in their finite forms. On the other hand, the repetitious, asyndetic use of verbs is impressionistic sketch-like writing:

> Then the beetle-shaped men come with their violins; wait; count; nod; down come their bows. (p. 116)

The abstract quality-nouns are employed, but not in any striking manner, as with the Goncourts. They are frequently, but not always, connected with visual images:

> The blankness of the white table-cloth glares. (p. 85)
> Now let us issue from the darkness of solitude. (p. 88)
> The swiftness of my mind is too strong for my body. (p. 92)

Contrary to the impressionistic devices of the Goncourts, Virginia Woolf does not particularly often resort to turning an adjective into a noun. What looks like a substantivized adjective, is mostly due to ellipsis or an unusual word-order:

> ... the many threads, the thin, the thick, the broken, the enduring of our long history. (p. 144)
> ... meadows of the rose, the crocus, of the rock and the snake too, of the sported and the swart; the embarrassing, the binding and tripping up. (p. 175)

On the other hand, she is very fond of the substantivized ing-forms in the plural — also an impressionistic device:

> I hear tramplings, tremblings, stirrings round me. (p. 8)
> ... after its listenings, and its waitings, and its suspicions. (p. 128)

... all these callings hither and thither, these pluckings and searchings. (p.
158—9)

...these greetings, recognitions, pluckings of the finger and searchings of the
eye. (p. 164)

Participles and gerunds add effectively to spatial-temporal nuances.
As they will be treated more fully in a later section, one example of
their use may suffice here:

Then there is the being eviscerated — drawn out, spun like a spider's web
and twisted in agony round a thorn. (p. 177)

c. Free adjuncts[1])

The previous example brings us to a very prominent feature in
The Waves, the use of the free adjunct, which often, but not necessarily, contains a participle, with or without a conjunction.

Transfixed, stopped dead, I thought, 'I cannot interfere with a single stroke
of those brooms'. (pp. 170—1)
So, swinging my stick, with my eyes filmed, not with pride, but with humility
rather, I walked down the street. (p. 180)
... we waited for his approval, seldom given. (p. 173)

The detached position of any word or expression, either at the end or
at the beginning of the sentence is for the sake of emphasis connected
with rhythmical arrangements, often together with ellipsis.

Unhappy, unfriended, in exile he would sometimes, in moments of confidence,
describe how the surf swept over the beaches of his home. (p. 173)
There was the morning, fine; there was the afternoon, walking. (p. 58)
Up they bubble — images. (p. 27)
To be contracted by another person into a single being — how strange. (p. 64)
The voice petered out in the dome, wailing. (p. 200)
What dirty tricks it plays us, one moment free; the next, this. (p. 207)
I am about to meet — what? (p. 52)

d. Attributive clauses

The syntactical feature of tying in a knot, as it were, the different
threads that have appeared in the sentence, especially through the use
of consecutive attributive clauses, has been called by M. Deutschbein
»geballt impressionistisch».[2])

I have to recall things gone far, gone deep, sunk into this life or that and
become part of it; dreams, too, things surrounding me, and the inmates, those

---

[1]) Cf. later p. 87
[2]) *Neuenglische Stilistik*, p. 155

old half-articulate ghosts, who keep up their hauntings by day and night; who turn over in their sleep, who utter their confused cries, who put out their phantom fingers and clutch at me as I try to escape — shadows of people one might have been; unborn selves. (p. 205)

B. FIGURES

a. I n v e r s i o n   a n d   e l l i p s i s can be counted among structural devices as well as rhetorical figures. In *The Waves* they serve an emotional purpose and are best considered in that light. The inversion of subject and predicate is not frequent. It is mostly to be met with verbs denoting movement and with 'to be'.

> Here come warm gusts . . . (p. 16)
> Down showers the day . . . (p. 19)
> Up goes the rocket . . . (p. 84)
> Out rush a bristle of horned suspicions . . . (p. 178)
> Clear cut and unequivocal am I, too. (p. 118)
> Here am I shedding one of my life-skins . . . Here am I marching up and down this terrace alone . . . (p. 134)

With other verbs it is employed to focus heavily emotional attention to a particular word or expression:

> Into this crashed death — Percival's. (p. 186)

An unusual word-order (in rhetoric called *hyperbaton*) is in general one of the dominant traits of *The Waves*. A few examples must suffice here, as it has been given attention in other connections.

> On they roll, on they gallop; after hounds, after footballs. (p. 66)
> Of story, of design, I do not see a trace then. (p. 169)

Ellipsis and hyperbaton were seen together in the examples above on page 70. Ellipses appear in *The Waves* in great numbers (several times on most of the pages, on 87 pages out of 211, to be exact).

Ellipsis is often connected with *exclamation*. Homén[1]) divides exclamation into three sub-categories: 1. the emotional exclamation *(O Death!)* 2. ellipsis *(never again!)* 3. aposiopesis, a sentence begun but not finished *(O, then the agony — then the intolerable despair . . .)*. These are figures much favoured by the romantics in their time and it is natural that Virginia Woolf, too, should employ them in abundance, as they convey something of an immediate, spontaneous reaction of the sensibilities.

---

[1]) *op. cit.*, p. 301

b. A p o s t r o p h e   a n d   e x c l a m a t i o n are in close connection with each other helping to create vividness of representation. The silent soliloquy is made 'loud' and given a sense of actuality and excitement through the imperative forms.

> Look! Do not move. Grasp the ferns tight on the top of the wall. (p. 12)
> But observe how meretricious the phrase is — made up of what evasions and old lies. (p. 95)

The soliloquy is throughout the book enlivened through the elements of dialogue. The presence of the other characters is made felt, although we never hear the answers or reactions to the questions, apostrophes, and asides that abound.

> ... the pretence, the vulgarity of life (because I love it) shoots at you as I throw — catch it — my poem. (p. 64)

Mostly the apostrophes are addressed to people. 'Lord', 'Heaven', are occasionally used in the manner of a prayer:

> Oh, Lord, let them pass. Lord, let them ... (p. 8)

or else in a colloquial manner, in an exclamation:

> Lord, how pleasant! Lord, how good! (p. 186)
> Heaven be praised for solitude ... (p. 209)

Apostrophe and exclamation are sometimes employed for the sake of pathos connected with abstract concepts like Life, Death, Friendship, the dominating spiritual forces in the novel.

> O friendship, I too will press flowers between the pages of Shakespeare's sonnets! O friendship, how piercing are your darts — there, there, again there. (p. 64)

That is the youthful Bernard in all his high-falutin but self-ironical sentimentality. And this is Rhoda, the agonized and humourless soul:

> Oh, life, how I have dreaded you ... oh, human beings, how I have hated you. (p. 145)

Bernard's last words in the novel are meant to convey the whole emotional weight of the novel; their sound has a bathetic ring:

> Against you, I will fling myself, unvanquished and unyielding, O Death! (p. 211)

c. In q u e s t i o n s, which are employed in great numbers to give variety and the sense of a Now, pronominal direct forms predominate,with *what*-questions in the lead, *verbal ('am I . , , ?')* as the second, *who, why,* and *elliptical (They want a plot, do they? They want a reason?)* questions in fairly equal numbers as the third group. As to content, *colloquial (why can I not finish the letter I am writing?) rhetorical (I will gather my flowers and present them — Oh! to whom?; 'Are we not acceptable, moon?) philosophic ('What am I? I ask. This?; 'Who am I?)* questions are fairly evenly divided, the rhetorical question being in the minority. All three correspond to the different moods of the novel: the colloquial, the emotional, and the questioning, and cover the whole range from the trivial to the significant that the author aims at presenting.

d. The p a r e n t h e t i c a l c l a u s e is a handy means to impart information and establish the milieu. It is separated by commas, dashes, or brackets, sometimes by both dashes and brackets:

> ... I might have been, who knows, perhaps anything. (p. 95)
> But now disembodied, passing over fields without lodgment — (there is a river; a man fishes; there is a spire, there is the village street with its bow-windowed inn) — all is dreamlike and dim to me. (p. 48)

Sometimes one hears the author's own voice giving information and expressing personal opinions:

> I think sometimes (I am not twenty yet) I am not a woman, but the light that falls on this gate, on this ground. (pp. 70—1)
> They have made all the days of June — this is the twenty-fifth — shiny and orderly ... (p. 29)
> He unfastens his sock suspenders (let us be trivial, let us be intimate). (p. 36)
> ... some reflections apparently casual but full of profundity (profound criticism is often written casually) about some book I have been reading ... (pp. 56—7)
> I feel, as I look from the window, parting the curtains, 'That would give him no pleasure; but it rejoices me'! (We use our friends to measure our own stature.) (p. 65)

Within the silent soliloquy the parenthetical clause is a link between the simultaneous outer and inner happenings. Movement, sights, sounds, registered by the soliloquizing mind and the parallel meditation can thus be revealed interlocked, as on p. 68, describing Louis having his meal in a City restaurant.

C. SILENT SOLILOQUY

The silent soliloquy in *The Waves* is a combination of interior stream of consciousness with external action described and with an audience assumed, conducted on a normal lingual level. As the reader is allowed to enter into the minds of the characters, direct speech is used throughout, with 'I' and 'my' for pronouns. Occasionally, but very seldom, when other people's thoughts are recorded, a snatch of the *style indirect libre, erlebte Rede,* is inserted:

> 'If he had a son like that,' he was thinking, 'he would manage to send him to Oxford.' (p. 50)

The interludes are throughout in the past tense, forming a contrast to the changing tenses of the soliloquies. A time-bound phenomenon is juxtaposed with the 'time-redeemed' flux of the human consciousness. The present tense is used when immediate sense-perceptions and the mind's reaction to them are described, as on pages 7—8, with the children registering sights and sounds. But the normal changes of tenses are taken up to express past-present-future relations. In fact, the different tense-relations are very carefully taken into consideration, with infinitive, gerund and participle formations to add to subtle nuances. But the dominating tense is the *Now.* In his summing-up Bernard, reminiscing, uses also the past tenses, but as they reveal something that is contained in his consciousness, succession changes into co-existence and time loses its customarily accepted qualities appearing as something irreal, always in the Now. One is reminded of the image of a weaver, employed by Rivarol[1]): »Le mouvement entre deux repos est l'image du présent entre le passé est l'avenir. Le tisserand qui *fait* sa toile *fait* toujours ce qui n'est pas.» Time remains a mysterious quality, 'c'est qui n'est pas', mere movement.

Impressionistic writing, like impressionism in painting, reflects the combined interest in what is perceived and in the manner of perception, the artistic creation. The impressionist is counted among realists whose attention is given to the phenomenon and to its registering and analyzing, with the mind seen as a reflector. But for Virginia Woolf the mind is also a projector, as shown by her imagery. Side by side with the realist who relies on the impression there exists in her the romantic, the projector of emotions, the expressionist.

EXPRESSIONISM AND SYMBOLISM

Although *The Waves* has been termed the most expressionistic of Virginia Woolf's books, there is not very much to be added here on this point, for expressionism, in its widest meaning, has obliquely been dealt with especially in the first two chapters, where the attitudes and valua-

---

[1]) quoted by BEDA ALLEMANN in *Hölderlin und Heidegger*, p. 216

tions of the novel, its pattern and symbolism, its characterization and allegory, with the typical stressed and the individual suppressed, were discussed. Hyperbole, similes and metaphors, ubiquitous in *The Waves*, are also common ground for both manners of approach.

The projection of emotions, an expressionistic trait, appears in descriptive details when, for instance, inner states are compared with nature *(innocent landscapes)* or when nature is invested with feelings *(an uneasy flame; unhappy waves)*. Animism, which can also be counted among impressionistic devices,[1]) reflects a naïve phantasy-play, a romantic attitude *(chattering grey stones; sleep curls; corn sighs; leaves tossed in agony)* Personification is fairly rare in the imagery of *The Waves* *(the bleared eyes of blue glass; the stupid voice of the telephone; the trams and and omnibuses roared in the street)*, but on the symbolic level of description Death appears as the dominant background personality of the novel, the supreme object of personification.

Verbs, it was above pointed out, characterize the expressionistic style, substantives the impressionistic. So much of the use of the verbs in *The Waves* is for word-painting and rhythm that it is difficult to place them as such in either impressionistic or expressionistic categories:

> Then he got up and went; we all got up; we all went. But I, pausing, looked at the tree, and as I looked in autumn at the fiery and yellow branches, some sediment formed; I formed; a drop fell; I fell — that is, from some completed experience I had emerged. (pp. 179—180)
> Up and up it comes, approaches, hesitates, stops at my door. I cry, 'Come in. Sit by me. Sit on the edge of the chair.' Swept away by the old hallucination, I cry, 'Come closer, closer.' (p. 142)

Extreme expressionism likes to mutilate syntax and break grammatical rules. There is nothing of that in *The Waves* besides some catachretic sentences.[2])

Expressionism was a continuation of the symbolist movement. In the nineteen-twenties Roger Fry was translating Mallarmé's poetry into Eng-

---

[1]) Cf. ULLMANN, *op. cit.*, p. 142, on the impressionism of the Goncourts.

[2]) Virginia Woolf has definite views on the fashion: »The literary convention of the time is so artificial ... that, naturally, the feeble are tempted to outrage, and the strong are led to destroy the very foundations and rules of literary society. Signs of this are everywhere apparent. Grammar is violated; syntax disintegrated; as a boy staying with an aunt for the week-end rolls in the geranium bed out of sheer desperation as the solemnities of the sabbath wear out. (*The Captain's Death-Bed*, pp. 108—9).

lish. His enthusiasm made the literary discussions in Bloomsbury often centre round symbolist writing. Virginia Woolf must have felt attracted, though there are no essays on the symbolists in her collections, nor are there passages on them in the *Diary*, but, then, she did not deal explicitly with poetry in her essays. All the same, there is a striking affinity between her own art and that of the symbolists. In its nature the symbolist poetry was pre-eminently lyrical, aiming at catching the fleeting moment. Wolfgang Kayser points out[1]) how Mallarmé in his *L' Après midi d'un Faune* attempted to weave together the past and the present in the manner later to be taken up by Proust, Virginia Woolf, and Faulkner.

The characteristic features of symbolism, well known though they are, are worth enumerating in this connection, for all along they fit in with what Virginia Woolf was trying to do in her own field. For the first, the symbolists were particularly interested in the creative act.[2]) E. A. Poe's *Philosophy of Composition* and *The Raven* were their favourite reading, doing pioneer work for their own orientation. They believed in deliberate and careful creation in the manner of Poe, and made a conscious effort to find a new language which would open up a new reality, which also became the 'reality' of Virginia Woolf. They paid particular attention therefore to the manner and the medium of poetry. They believed in 'correspondances', in a mysterious ultimate unity of things, which was in their writing reflected in synaesthesia. Rhythm became specially important, with repetition and other devices to heighten the effect. Alliteration and the general musicality of sound contributed to the suggestiveness of the language. Metaphysical speculation concerning the position of the 'I' in the order of existence, and a feeling of the vagueness and uncertainty of all existence and of the world around, were characteristic attitudes. Virginia Woolf is constantly asking those questions through Bernard: 'Who am I? This. No, I am that.' Bernard sees human beings 'with blurred edges', vague pantheism prevails, in the symbolist manner. Vagueness is in *The Waves* expressed through adjectives rather than the use of the indefinite pronouns. Disembodied, ephemeral, floating, immeasurable, inarticulate, indefinite, insignificant,

---

[1]) in his essay on Der europäische Symbolismus, *Vortragsreise*, p. 293.

[2]) So were the impressionists, for that matter. As has been pointed out by Ortega y Gasset and others (cf. ULLMANN, *op. cit.*, p. 137), impressionism had the tendency of becoming abstract with attention shifted from phenomena to the act of perception.

interminable, undifferentiated, unidentified, unsubstantial, vague, vanishing, etc., are some of the typical and recurrent epithets.

The 'reality' of anything can only be reached through suggestions and
its former mythical power, and must be freed, as Kayser points out in his
essay, from the ties of Now and Here as well as from the bondage of the
speaking I. All this is exactly what Virginia Woolf was aiming at especially in *The Waves*. Symbolism, rather than expressionism, is the
term to be applied to her art.

5. SENTENCE AND RHYTHM

Rhythm was an important aspect for the Symbolists. In a passage
of *The Waves* (p. 57) Virginia Woolf implies what she expressly says in
A Letter to a Young Poet[1]), namely, that rhythm, 'the most profound
and primitive of instincts', is the basic element in the creative process.
Rhuthmós precedes *Logos*.[2]) In her theorizing she is as vague as is Edgar
Allan Poe in his definition of the poetry of words as 'The Rhythmical
Creation of Beauty'[3]). but both attempt to illustrate the problem in
practice, especially in *The Raven* and in *The Waves*.

> Now begins to rise in me the familiar rhythm, words that have lain dormant
> now lift, now toss their crests and fall and rise, and fall and rise again. (p. 59)

The imagery here as elsewhere in the novel points to the basic connection
of *rhuthmós* with *rhein*, to flow.[4]) This element of movement is kept up not
only by the recurrence of larger patterns, of certain rhetorical devices and
syntactical arrangements but also by the choice of grammatical forms,
especially those of the verbs, the natural media of action. Words wag
and flick their tails, they move through the air in flocks

> now this way, now that way, moving all together, now dividing, now coming
> together. (pp. 14—15)

---

[1]) *Op. cit.*, p. 140.

[2]) LUDVIG KLAGES, in *Vom Wesen des Rhythmus*, sees rhythm as part of the
basic, as yet unconscious experience, and distinguishes rhythm from metre on
the basis of consciousness, involved in the latter. This is what Virginia Woolf
also seems to imply. Clive Bell speaks of 'the all-pervading rhythm that informs all
things' (*Art*, p. 57), and juxtaposes 'the essential reality', 'the God in everything',
'the universal in the particular', 'the all-pervading rhythm' (ibid. p. 169). This
sounds like something that Virginia Woolf, too, could have said.

[3]) *Tales, Poems, Essays*, Collins Classics, p. 491.

[4]) SUSANNE K. LANGER, *op. cit.*, p. 128, points to the dynamic character of
a breaking wave, its true Gestalt quality.

The ing-forms, with their variety and range of syntactical possibilities, offer fine opportunities for rhythmical exploitation. Their position in *The Waves* is so striking — well over two thousand cases — that they tempt one to a closer investigation of how they have been exploited. In view of their many-sided employment, a schematic arrangement seems advisable. Attention is in the following discussion given both to grammatical and rhetorical aspects and the examples have been chosen accordingly.[1])

THE ING-FORMS

I. PURE NOUNS AND ADJECTIVES

The p u r e l y n o m i n a l f o r m s, *beginning, meaning, calling, blessing, foreboding, lodging,* etc., are numerous, constituting as they do a normal element of both referential and emotive language, to use I. A. Richards's perhaps over-simplified but useful and convenient categories. *Being* and *feeling* are, characteristically, the most often repeated words of this type. Besides the gerundial and participial uses, *being* as a pure substantive has been used in its four meanings: 1. e x i s t e n c e, s t a t e o f e x i s t i n g (Things quiver as if not yet in being; unmoored as I am from a private being; this intensity of being; this veil, sense of being;) 2. a h u m a n c r e a t u r e, l i v i n g p e r s o n (a single and passing being; the whole being; the complete human being; the being grows rings like a tree;) 3. e s s e n c e, n a t u r e (this edge, curve, spring of being; I took my mind, my being, the old dejected, almost inanimate object . . .;). The nuances are often vague, No. 1 and No. 3 being in some cases interchangeable (the order, roof, spring of my being). In its fourth meaning, h u m a n l i f e, *being* is, as far as I can see, to be understood in one sentence only; *the need I had to offer my being to one god,* and there, too, it is rather ambiguous, interchangeable with meaning No. 1. *Existence,* rather than *life,* is the key-word.

In the c o m p o u n d f o r m a t i o n s, also numerous, the gerundial element is more common than the participial (ger.: dining-room, eating-shop, meeting-place, sleeping-house, dwelling-place, dressing-

---

[1]) For further examples see *Ing-forms in the service of rhythm and style in Virginia Woolf's The Waves,* Bulletin of the Modern Language Association Helsinki, 1 LXI, 1960

gown, crossing-sweeper, railway cutting, etc.; part.: downfalling, wire-fencing, circulating library, sporting column). There is some discrepancy in hyphenation: both *looking glass* and *looking-glass*, *well-being* and *wellbeing* appear in the text.

The p u r e l y a d j e c t i v a l forms, like *harrowing, astonishing, appalling*, etc., used both as attributes and predicatives, offer few deviations from the ordinary usage. Of a d v e r b i a l use, not very common in literary English anyway, there is only one example with some adverbial element in it:

> Now the stab, the rent in my defences that Neville made with his astonishing fine rapier, is repaired. (p. 65)

The abundant use of g e r u n d s and p r e s e n t p a r t i c i p l e s offers ample material for illustrating practically speaking all of their varied roles in the English language.

II. GERUND

A. USED WITH THE SYNTACTICAL PROPERTIES OF A NOUN

I. Combined with other words

a) preceded by an article

Antithetical coupling and the repetitive element are often included:

> ... the grinding and the steam that runs in unequal drops down the window pane; and the stopping and the starting with a jerk of motor-omnibuses ... (p. 68)
>
> There was a drawing in of chairs and a drawing out of chairs on the linoleum. (p. 90)

Visual and auditory effects are conveyed, the ing-form strengthening the impressionistic character of the description:

> For one day as I leant over a gate that led into a field, the rhythm stopped; the rhymes and the hummings, the nonsense and the poetry. (p. 201)
>
> There is a dancing and a drumming, like the dancing and the drumming of naked men with assagais. (p. 100)

b) preceded by a pronoun

1. possessive

> Therefore I go, dubious, but elate; apprehensive of intolerable pain; yet I think bound in my adventuring to conquer after huge suffering ... (p. 44)

I am most grateful to you men in black and you, dead, for your leading. (p. 42)

I have seen clouds cover the stars, then free the stars, then cover the stars again. Now I look at their changing no more. (p. 209)

(*But: look at us trooping after him; imagine him undressing;* the participial form with an accusative stresses the descriptive element.) *Vanishing* in *the sight of her vanishing* could be either gerund or participle, but with the action in progress, the latter, used predicatively (cf. below p. 85) seems more natural. In *that is my saving; solitude is my undoing* the gerunds are being used in the passive sense and the possessive is the subject part of the nexus.[1]) An often-repeated combination of imagery, rhetorical devices and rhythm is present in the following passage:

But heat and cold will follow each other naturally with my willing or unwilling. My children will carry me on; their teething, their crying, their going to school and coming back will be like the waves of the sea under me. (p. 94)

2. other pronouns

After all these callings hither and thither, these pluckings and searchings, I shall fall alone through this thin sheet into gulfs of fire. (pp. 158—9)

I, I, I, tired as I am, spent as I am, an almost worn out with all this rubbing of my nose along the surfaces of things . . . (p. 210)

c) preceded by a noun in the genitive

Only one example occurs in the text, with a proper noun (*Jinny's pirouetting*). The predominance of accusatives is in keeping with the grammatical rule.[2]) As the text of *The Waves* is impressionistically descriptive and repetition is one of its main features, it is only natural that accusatives, mostly with participles, should abound.[3]) The stress on the importance of the direct sensuous awareness of the world around us is also reflected in this syntactical connection in that the subject with the gerunds, whether animate or inanimate, is, except for this one example, in the accusative. The stylized colloquialism — if one may coin such a term — also makes the preference of the accusative form seem natural.

d) preceded by an adjective

The wealth of adjectives is characteristic of Virginia Woolf's style in general; their appearing with the gerunds is in harmony with the general trend:

---

1) cf. JESPERSEN, *Essentials of English Grammar*, p. 322.

2) cf. CURME *Syntax*, pp. 485 ff., and JESPERSEN, *op. cit.* p. 324.

3) cf. below Bc, p. 82, cf. also Participle Ba & b, pp. 85—6

I have heard threads broken and knots tied and the quiet stitching of white cambric going on and on on the knees of a woman. (p. 141)

... the turf is trodden bare by our incessant unmethodical pacing. (p. 193)

Their quivering mackerel sparkling was darkened. (p. 53)

e) followed by a noun adjunct with a preposition *of* which is, naturally, the most common preposition in this connection:

Meanwhile let us abolish the ticking of time's clock with one blow. (p. 129)

There is only one example with another preposition:

the sucking at pipes (p. 191)

f) used as an adjunct to a predicative noun or adjective in sentences with what Zandvoort calls 'introductory', Curme 'anticipatory' and Jespersen 'preparatory' *it*.

This is a means to emphasize the adjective or noun in question. Although Virginia Woolf likes to find different ways of expressing emphasis and often uses *it* and *there* constructions to do so, there is only one example of this particular expression:

It is dull ... walking along the high road with no windows to look at ... (p. 17)

II. Functioning as a part of the sentence

a) subject

This talking is undressing an old woman whose dress had seemed to be part of her ... (p. 94)
Rippling and questioning begin. (p. 165)
Then there is the being eviscerated ... (p. 177)
There was the afternoon, walking. (p. 58)

b) object

Compared with the corresponding verbal forms, there are relatively few examples:

Time's fangs have ceased their devouring. (p. 162)
... they have given up calling for a self who does not come ... (p. 55)

c) nominal predicative

All is rippling, all is dancing; all is quickness and triumph. (p. 33)

d) part of a prepositional adjunct

In spite of his impatiently protesting that it did not matter ... (p. 187)

B. USED WITH THE SYNTACTICAL PROPERTIES OF A VERB

a) qualified by an adverb or an adverbial phrase

Nothing should be named lest by so doing we change it. (p. 59)
But Neville delicately avoiding interference ... (p. 65)

b) taking an object

Swaying and opening programmes, with a few words of greeting to friends,
we settle down ... (p. 115)

c) taking a subject of its own (cf. above A. 1. c. p. 80)

Not sighs and laughter; not circling and ingenuous phrases; not Rhoda's
strange communications when she looks past us, over our shoulders; nor
Jinny's pirouetting, all of a piece, limbs and body. (p. 71)

(This serves also as an example of a nominal, elliptical structure, which,
as we saw in the previous chapter, is typical of impressionistic writing.)

d) used in perfect tense

without having signalled;

e) in the passive voice

from being blown; far from being allowed;

C. VERBAL AND/OR SUBSTANTIVAL

a) as a part of a prepositional adjunct

and then tiring of pursuit and flight, lovelily they came descending, delicately
declining, dropped down and sat silent on the tree, on the wall, with their
bright eyes glancing, and their heads turned this way, that way. (p. 53)

— an example of how skilfully the author manipulates the ing-forms.
Alliteration, musical vowels and consonants, rhythmical and rhetorical arrangements contribute to the cadence.

b) as an object or adjunct to a number of verbs and verbal phrases,
of which *give up, cannot help, keep on, go on, stop, prevent (from), do
with* have been used in the text.

Of these verbs *keep on* and *go on* seem to have a special importance
in contributing to rhythmical and symbolic effects. Expressions like
people go on passing, the door keeps on opening are repeated in several
variations and combinations. They help in giving the impression of a
constant flow, symbolizing, so it seems to me, both the stream of consciousness and the streaming away of human life. The sentence, *The
door opens, the door goes on opening*, occurs five times (pp. 75, 86, 101,

111, 125), i.e. at fairly regular intervals, very often combined with
antithesis and parallelism (*doors will open and shut, will keep opening
and shutting*), which are the weft and warp in the texture of the symbolic
pattern of the novel. The verbs used to express all this continuous
going on are almost exclusively dynamic, denoting movement and
action themselves. Movement is thus added to movement.

The expressions of continuity and the descriptive passages of transitory
sense-impressions form a significant combination, creating tension
between the permanent, the wave-like going *and* returning — *the eternal
renewal, the incessant rise and fall and fall and rise again* (p. 211) —
and the evanescent, the present moment which vanishes into the stream
of time never to return as such, yet eternally present in the future.
Bergson's d u r é e — Virginia Woolf was interested in Bergson —
and, to allow oneself a fashionable point of comparison, Heidegger's
u r s p r ü n g l i c h e Z e i t l i c h k e i t[1]) come to mind in this connection. T. E. Eliot, in the opening lines of his *Four Quartets*, deals
with the same image.[2]

c) with *like*

As the language of *The Waves* is metaphorical, abounding in similes,
the reader encounters *as if* and *like* on every page, sometimes in nearly
every sentence of a page. In the gerundial constructions (*like swimmers
just touching the ground*) verbs denoting movement and action are a
prominent feature.

> *like* a cat returning, skaters rollicking, a torrent jumping, a mountain goat
> leaping, a dragon flying, a net descending, a net folding, hands closing, etc.
> (innumerable examples).

Auditory effects are more often combined, in the narrative sections,
than visual:

> like trees cracking, an old shell murmuring, the echo of voice laughing down; etc.

D. Gerund or infinitive

A comparison between the use of gerund and infinitive forms with verbs
that can take either shows that Virginia Woolf here[3]) prefers the infini-

---

[1]) cf. *Sein und Zeit*, p. 329

[2]) cf. also Yrjö Luojola on the stream of time, one of the leitmotifs of V. A.
Koskenniemi's poetry. Valvoja No. 3, 1959, pp. 88—97.

[3]) It is interesting to note that Marjatta Salo in her pro-gradu work (Helsinki University) on the use of the gerund in some of Virginia Woolf's earlier

tive, which underlines the studied informality of the language. In the only example of *begin* with the gerund (*Now the red boy begins firing at a pheasant*) repetition seems to be implied. In the twelve examples with the infinitive there are no deviations from normal usage:

> she begins to run; I begin to draw; etc.

In most of them it is a question of a particular act, instinctive rather than deliberate:

> Only, when I have lain alone on the hard ground, watching you play your game, I begin to feel the wish to be singled out; Now begins to rise in me the familiar rhythm; Cold water begins to run;

Against the one case of *cease* with a substantival gerund (*Time's fangs have ceased their devouring*), there are two sentences with the infinitive. *Continue* only appears with the infinitive, *hate* and *like* only with gerunds, *love* once with gerund (*They loved riding*), in three sentences with the infinitive:

> I love to hear the gong roar; I love punctually at ten to come into my room; I love to slip the virtue and severity;

There the distinction between a general and a particular occasion has been sustained.

III PRESENT PARTICIPLE

By far the greatest number of the ing-forms in *The Waves* are present participles. Stylistically they are of special importance in their role of forming abridged clauses, an important factor in giving the writing an impressionistic stamp.

A. USED WITH NOUNS

a) an attribute *before* the noun

There are over two hundred examples, of which over a hundred denote movement, over thirty, visual impressions, the rest conveying other sense impressions. *Scrolloping*, in *some scrolloping tomb* is obviously a neologism, a graphic one too, formed from the substantive *scroll*. The OED does not know of *scrollop*. *Obliterating satisfaction* in *my*

---

novels finds (p. 26 and 165) the gerund overwhelmingly dominant with *begin*. The variety at the author's disposal in *The Waves* is so great that there is no need to force a use of an ing-form, if it does not come effortlessly.

moment of obliterating satisfaction points, like the use of *devastating*, in *this devastating sense of grey ashes in a burnt grate; his devastating presence* to Virginia Woolf's fondness of hyperbolic language.

b) *after* the noun

1. predicative and semi-predicative

... the flight of doves descending ...
... multitudes of people suffering ...
... I find myself falling, fluttering, descending, and perching upon some curious gargoyle ...
Neville, scissor-cutting, exact;

There is variation in the hyphenation of the numerous compounds, adding to nuances of meaning:

the meadows primeval looking; (but: sensual-looking gentry); the tree was Byron's tree, lachrymose, down-showering, lamenting; flowers, green veined and quivering; (but: shell-veined)

2. attributive (together with an accompanying object or adjunct)

'Week-days are in it', said Susan, 'Monday, Tuesday, Wednesday; the horses going up to the fields, and the horses returning; the rooks rising and falling, and catching the elm-trees in their net, whether it is April, whether it is November.' (p. 104)

B. USED WITH CERTAIN VERBS

a) the accusative with present participle or infinitive, after *hear, feel, see, watch* (and other verbs of sense-perception)
As is natural in a text where sense-perceptions are made the starting-point for the mind's journey towards a 'total vision', the examples here are numerous. The ratio between participles and infinitives is roughly two to one, with the participles dominant. The durative element is accentuated:

Silence will close behind us. If I look back over that bald head, I can see silence already closing and the shadows of clouds chasing each other over the empty moor; silence closes over our transient passage. (p. 47)

Tenses are employed with an attention given to subtle temporal nuances. Participles and infinitives are also used to convey shades of implication. A durative and repetitive element in the former and that of an objective statement of fact in the latter, are implied in the following:

Looking-glasses confronted me in which I could see my pinioned body and people passing; stopping, looking, and going on indifferent. (p. 198)

(*But:* I have seen the lady powder her nose three times in the midst of an absorbing conversation. You see me take my napkin and unfold it. You see me pour myself out a glass of wine.)

As I drop asleep at night it strikes me sometimes that I shall never see savages in Tahiti spearing fish by the light of a blazing cresset, or a lion spring in the jungle, or a naked man eating raw flesh. (p. 132)

... I feel come over me the sense of the earth under me, and my roots going down and down till they wrap themselves round some hardness at the centre. (p. 25)

Sudden action expressed through the use of the infinitive, durative, descriptive implication by the participle, is a rule observed in the previous examples. With *hear*, too, the nuances are observed, but are perhaps not quite as clear as with *see* and *feel:*

We hear them *crying* with sharp, stag-like barks, 'Open, open' ... We hear the beech trees and the birch trees *raise* their branches ... (p. 163)

b) the accusative with present participle (without the alternative of infinitive)

Keep, leave, set appear in the text. Compared to *keep on* with gerund, the participle construction is rare. In the phrases *to go blackberrying, cricketing, footballing,* which occur in the text, the ing-form is a participle, with the ingressive aspect dominant, as it so often is in *The Waves,* adding to the dynamic character of the language.

C. USED AS A NOUN

The examples are few, mostly appearing in elliptical sentences, one of which may be quoted as an example of Virginia Woolf's tendency to condense to the point of unintelligibility.

Now through this transparency became visible those wondrous pastures, at first so moon-white, radiant, where no foot has been; meadows of the rose, the crocus, of the rock and the snake too; of the spotted and swart; *the embarrassing, the binding and tripping up.* (p. 175)

D. FORMING AN ABRIDGED CLAUSE

I. an equivalent to an Adverbial Clause[1]) used without a conjunction. Examples with manner and cause implied are by far the most numerous:

... he is somehow to be pitied, breasting the world with half-finished phrases, having lost his ticket: he is also to be loved (p. 51).

---

[1]) termed by CURME (*op. cit.* 177) 'the predicate appositive participial construction'.

Being naturally truthful, he did not see the point of these exaggerations . . .
(p. 111)
Now leaping, now lashing, they are laid on shore. (p. 164)

II. used in a Free Adjunct (practically equivalent to a co-ordinate
clause), so termed if there is a clear break between the participle construction and the rest of the sentence.

a) with or without a conjunction

The repeated use of present participles in Free Adjuncts contributes to
giving the language of *The Waves* a stylized stamp, and is one of the
most important factors in the formation of its rhythm, espically as
repetition is often combined with it. Their shifting place in the sentence
also adds to the impression of an advancing and receding movement:

> Opening and shutting, shutting and opening, with increasing hum and sturdi-
> ness, the haste and fever of youth are drawn into service until the whole being
> seems to expand in and out like the mainspring of a clock. (p. 183)

> Meeting and parting, we assemble different forms, make different patterns.
> (p. 121)
> Having dropped off satisfied like a child from the breast, I am at liberty now
> to sink down, deep, into what passes, this omnipresent, general life. (p. 81)

> Sitting alone, it seems we are spent. (p. 189)

b) used in an Absolute Participle Construction, where the participle
is preceded by a noun or a pronoun functioning as its subject[1])

> he burrowing like some vast cocoon meanwhile; I leaning slightly upon Jinny;

This group also contains a certain type of *with*-construction very
common in *The Waves:*

> I am stretched, among these long lights, these long waves, these endless paths,
> with people pursuing, pursuing. (p. 20)

The absolute participle construction through its nature greatly adds to
the vividness of style, making the sentences loose and flexible. The
loosest type, the unrelated participle construction where the present
participle does not refer to any particular word in the sentence that
can be considered its subject, only appears in one example:

> The youth in the corner, judging from the nervous way in which he puts his
> hand from time to time to the back of his head, is from the country. (p. 103)

---

[1]) CURME calls this 'the nominative absolute construction', *op. cit.* p. 153

E. Expanded Forms

Expanded forms can effectively be made to serve several purposes in descriptive and emotional contexts. Besides implying aspects concerning time, they can convey nuances of feeling. Where the static simple form expresses a fact objectively, unemotionally, the expanded form may convey satisfaction, happy or unhappy anticipation, praise or indignation, censure, displeasure or pleasure, etc., as the case may be. With continuity of action as their basic aspect, it is only natural that Virginia Woolf should have used them in abundance, as usual connected with other stylistic aspects.

> Now I am getting the hang of it. Now I am getting this beat into my brain (the rhythm is the main thing in writing). Now without pausing I will begin, on the very lilt of the stroke — —. (p. 57)

In the foregoing passage, pleasant expectation and an unfolding action which culminates in the 'I will' of the last sentence, can be seen as implied. The purely durative element is reflected in the following passage, the liveliness of description becoming at the same time greatly enhanced:

> They are listening to the gramophone; they are eating fruit out of paper bags·
> They are tossing the skins of bananas, which then slink eel-like, into the river·
> (p. 59)

Transitoriness is implied in:

> ... all the drops are sparkling, trembling, as if the garden were a splintered mosaic, vanishing, twinkling; (p. 175)

A certain leisureliness:

> You have been reading Byron. You have been marking the passages that seem to approve of your own character. (p. 62)

Informality of expression:

> He must be passing some shop; / Somebody must be seeing him now.

Simultaneity:

> And while you gesticulate, with your cloak, your cane, I am trying to expose a secret told to nobody yet; I am asking you (as I stand with my back to you) to take my life in your hands — —;

Hyberbole gets its due also in this connection:

> I am for ever sleeping and waking; / We are forever mixing ourselves with unknown quantities;

An ingressive element is often implied and the descriptive force increased:

> The door is opening and shutting. People are arriving; / Now, too, the time is coming when we shall leave school and wear long skirts. Life is beginning.

Anticipation and pleasure were implied in the previous; an iterative aspect is obvious in the following sentence:

> They are always forming into fours and marching in troops;

Displeasure is an element in the following quotation, said by Neville, the intellectual, about Percival, the athlete:

> He is thinking of nothing but the match.

Certainty of fulfilment is expressed with 'going to':

> It is going to be a brilliant sketch which, she must think, was written without a pause, without an erasure.

Futurity with certain nuances, intention, plan, near future, can also be found in the following examples:

> This is the place to which he is coming; / »Percival is going», said Neville. »We sit here — —; / Miss Curry is taking us for a brisk walk, while Miss Hudson sits at her desk settling her accounts.

With a conscious artist like Virginia Woolf, an abundance of ing-forms, such as there is in *The Waves*, is not just a rather irritating stylistic trick, but part and parcel of the *significant form*. The nervous speed and rush in *The Waves*, the lilt and the billowing of the rhythm, are graphically transferred to the reader's consciousness specially through the use of the ing-forms. There is hardly another work of art in English where they have been used in as varied, effective and illustrative manner, their possibilities, rhythmical and syntactical, having been taken advantage of to the full.

ANTITHESIS AND OTHER DEVICES

Thematic antitheses have been discussed in the earlier chapters: reality — 'reality', the evanescent phenomenon — the permanent pattern, the limited time of the clock — the unlimited time of the mind, the every-day existence — higher states of consciousness, the present moment — eternity, the unsatisfactory reality — the visionary life, the loftiness of human aspiration — the inadequacy of achievement. *Anticlimax* is connected with the shock-technique, the juxtaposing of the elevated and the trivial, of which examples have been given in

several connections in this study. Of *chiasmus* in its pure form, with
inversion, there are no examples. *Antimetabolism, anaclasis, punning,
oxymoron, epigrams, innuendo,* are not represented in their unambiguous
forms either. Humour appears occasionally, *irony* hardly at all, perhaps
because *The Waves* is meant to speak to emotions rather than to intellect.

Examples of antithetical arrangement of words and images are to be
counted in hundreds. The most recurrent are, again, light images (sun-
shadow, light — dark, dawn — dusk, day — night, etc.) and abstract
ideas (life — death, beauty — ugliness, love — hate, chaos — order, etc.).
Of verbs those denoting motion are, as is to be expected, the most
common: fall — rise, shut — open, expand — contract, meet — part,
run — pause, stop — start, etc.:

> Lifts rise and fall; trains stop, trains start as regularly as the waves of the
> sea. (p. 139)

Adjectives follow suit: 'laughing yet desperate', remote — close, 'not
one and simple but complex and many', etc., in great variety.

> There are many rooms — many Bernards. There was the charming, but weak;
> the strong, but supercilious; the brilliant, but remorseless; the very good
> fellow, but, I make no doubt, the awful bore; the sympathetic, but cold; the
> shabby, but — go into the next room — the foppish, worldly, and too well
> dressed. What I was to myself was different; was none of these. (p. 184)

Adverbs, pronouns, conjunctions, and negatives appear in numerous
pairs of contrast: entirely — not at all, this — that, with — without,
everybody — nobody; »They say, 'Yes', they say, 'No'», etc.

Antithesis is frequently combined with other stylistic devices, most
often with those of repetition, very effective in contributing to the
wave-like movement of the rhythm:

> we are all deeply moved; yet irreverent; yet penitent; yet anxious to get it
> over; yet reluctant to part. (p. 43)

Repetition, with anaphora and epiphora, asyndeton and polysyndeton,
parallelism, accumulation, and word-order, with the detached adjunct
given a prominent position, are, as pointed out earlier, the main
rhythmical devices:

> The sound of the chorus came across the water and I felt leap up that old
> impulse, which has moved me all my life, to be thrown up and down on the
> roar of other people's voices, singing the same song; to be tossed up and down
> on the roar of almost senseless merriment, sentiment, triumph, desire. But
> not now. No! I could not collect myself; I could not distinguish myself; I
> could not help letting fall the things that had made me a minute ago eager,

amused, jealous, vigilant, and hosts of other things, into the water. I could not recover myself from that endless throwing away, dissipation, flooding forth without our willing it and rushing soundlessly away out there under the arches of the bridge, round some clump of trees or an island, out where sea-birds sit on stakes, over the roughened water to become waves in the sea — could not recover myself from that dissipation. So we parted. (p. 198)

Rhythmically, this is a characteristic passage. First there is tension and upward movement with the sense of excitement: 'The sound . . . desire.' Then the slowing down: 'But not now. No.', after which follows an accumulation of repetitions and amplifications of the theme, until a dramatic and abrupt summing-up binds the rambling thoughts together. It is truly as if a wave rolled on till it reached the shore.

It is interesting to follow the account in Virginia Woolf's *Diary* of the development of the theme. The novel was to be called The Moths, but the waves-imagery started to force itself to the foreground. At the beginning of 1929 the author began wondering: 'Could one not get the waves to be heard through?' By June that year the waves had gained supremacy. The reply to the author's question must be in the affirmative. The novel could not have been given a better name than *The Waves*.

CHAPTER IV

CONCLUSION

The Waves is an account of a private and inner experience, transferable into words with great difficulty, if at all. It is not about what life is like or human beings are like — the characters remain 'humours' intentionally. It is not about the world around us either. It is an account of a creative vision, of the artist's approach to reality and his experience of 'reality'. There is no better explanation for this mysterious concept which appears so often both in Virginia Woolf's *Diary* and in this study, than the one Clive Bell gives in the chapter called *The Metaphysical Hypothesis*[1]) According to it, 'the ultimate reality' corresponds to Kant's 'das Ding an sich' and in art is to be seen behind and through 'significant form'. The artist has a peculiar talent, through his mental and emotional power, his imagination, to catch this reality and give it an

---

[1]) *op. cit.*, p. 54.

expression through 'pure form'. Concentrating on visual arts, Bell speaks of lines and colours but includes, mutatis mutandis, every type of artistic creation. In *To the Lighthouse* and *The Waves*, more explicitly than in her other novels, Virginia Woolf illustrates the same problems that Clive Bell and Roger Fry are dealing with in their essays. She elucidates the artist's vision from her own angle and with the means at her disposal, as a practising artist who speaks of what she knows from experience but what is all the same very difficult to express in words and can perhaps only be expressed through symbols and allegory.

It is interesting to see how Virginia Woolf's basic dichotomy is reflected in *The Waves* all along. She appears both as a romantic and a realist, a believer in irrational forces and intuition in her manner of creation, yet a rationalist who relies on the testimony of the senses; an impressionist with an interest primarily in phenomena and an expressionist with a belief in the symbolic as the ultimate reality.

Virginia Woolf was a conscious and conscientious craftsman, for whom intuition was only a starting-point in creation. In fact, *The Waves*, while it describes the share of intuition, was itself composed — not without intuition but with an overwhelming share of deliberate, even laborious effort, written and re-written several times. The Diary allows us to see that the design of the novel was at the start almost non-existent. The novel started vaguely as 'an abstract mystical eyeless book; a playpoem.'[1]) Then the design began to formulate itself, and the Gestalt-formation decreed the growth, with the waves as the central image and rhythm as the dominant figure, really an 'all-pervading' element. With the symbolic and the story levels interacting, *The Waves* turns out to be all of a piece, coherent and integrated, with vision and language in harmony, with content and form as an inseparable whole. The allegorical 'meaning' is subdued to form an undercurrent, enriching, not disturbing the organism of the whole.

Admittedly *The Waves* is a *tour de force*, as a novel an interesting experiment rather than an unqualified success. All the same it is a valuable achievement as a work of art, for through it something important has been conveyed into words, expressed in an original manner. It is a reflection of a sensitive and modern mind — quite as modern as T. S. Eliot's, though Virginia Woolf concentrates on studying the fertility of the human consciousness rather than the sterility of

---

[1]) *Diary*, p. 137, 7. 11. 1928.

modern society. *The Four Quartets* and *The Waves* have mutual affinity; *The Waste Land* is an alien country. The source of frustration, if such there was, and undoubtedly there was, lay for Virginia Woolf in the falling short of artistic perfection, not in the discrepancy between life and art.

The Waves proves better than any other work by Virginia Woolf to what extent her life was dedicated to art. The absence of all questions as irrelevant that trouble a Thomas Mann or a T. S. Eliot, say, about art-life relationship, results in the absence also of envigorating tensions and of the torturing irony that adds to the value of those writers. Virginia Woolf's world is the proverbial ivory tower of a dedicated artist, whose contribution to life and fulfilment of social duty lies in the passionate concentration on finding an expression for something individual and private. Suggestion and evocation, the best, perhaps the only, means to convey this kind of experience, have in *The Waves* been made the principles to which language and style have been subjected. The novel cannot be denied unity. The realization of its vision, though forced, shows how far a language-conscious author can stretch the limits of expression outside the realm of poetry.

BIBLIOGRAPHY

A. Books by Virginia Woolf, quoted or referred to in this study:

The Voyage Out, 1915
Night and Day, 1938 (1919)
Jacob's Room, 1947 (1922)
Mrs. Dalloway, 1947 (1925)
The Common Reader, First Series, 1948 (1925)
To the Lighthouse, 1946 (1927)
Orlando, 1949 (1928)
A Room of One's Own, 1946 (1929)
The Waves, 1950 (1931)
A Letter to a Young Poet, 1932
The Years, 1937
Three Guineas, 1947 (1938)
Roger Fry, 1940
The Death of the Moth and Other Essays, 1947 (1942)
The Captain's Death-Bed and Other Essays, 1950
A Writer's Diary, 1953 (ed. by Leonard Woolf)
For a further list of Virginia Woolf's works as well for reference books concerning her personality and milieu, see *Virginia Woolf and Bloomsbury*, pp. 161–7. (Annales Academiae Scientiarum Fennicae, B 82, 1) Helsinki 1953.

B. Sources and Reference Books:

ABENIUS, MARGIT, *Stilstudier i Kellgrens prosa*. Uppsala, 1931.
ABRAMS, M. H., *The Mirror and the Lamp*. Romantic Theory and the Critical Tradition, New York, 1953.
ALLEMANN, BEDA, *Hölderlin und Heidegger*. Zürich u. Freiburg, 1954.
ARISTOTLE's *Poetics and Rhetoric*. Everyman's Library No. 901. London, 1953.
ARMSTRONG, EDWARD A., *Shakespeare's Imagination*. London, 1946.
BADENHAUSEN, I., *Die Sprache Virginia Woolfs*. Diss., Marburg, 1932.
BARTLETT, JOHN, *A Complete Concordance* or verbal index to words, phrases, and passages in the dramatic works of Shakespeare. London, 1953.
BELL, CLIVE, *Art*. London, 1949 (1914)
—»— *Proust*. London, 1928.
BJÖRK, STAFFAN, *Studier in prosaberättarens teknik*. Romanens formvärld. Stockholm, 1953.
BODELSEN, C. A., *T. S. Eliot's Four Quartets*. A Commentary. Copenhagen, 1958.

BOWRA, C. M., *The Creative Experiment*. London, 1949.

BROOKE-ROSE, CHRISTINE, *A Grammar of Metaphor*. London, 1958.

BROWNE, SIR THOMAS, *Religio Medici*. Everyman's Library No. 92. London, 1956.

BYRON, LORD GEORGE GORDON, *The Poetical Works of Lord Byron*. Oxford, 1952.

BÖCKMANN, PAUL (ed.), *Stil- und Formprobleme in der Literatur*. Vorträge des VIII. Kongresses der Internationalen Vereinigung für moderne Sprachen und Literaturen in Heidelberg. Heidelberg, 1959.

CASSIRER, ERNST, *An Essay on Man*. An Introduction to a Philosophy of Human Culture. New York, 1954 (1944).

—»— *Language and Myth*. New York, 1946.

CHIARI, JOSEPH, *Symbolism from Poe to Mallarmé*. The Growth of a Myth. London, 1957.

CLEMEN, WOLFGANG, *The Development of Shakespeare's Imagery*. London, 1953 (1951)

COLERIDGE, S. T., *Biographia Literaria*. Everyman's Library No. 11. London, 1956.

COOPER, LANE. (ed.), *A Concordance to the Poems of William Wordsworth*. London, 1911.

CROCE, BENEDETTO, *Aesthetic*. Transl. by D. Ainslie. New York, 1953.

CURME, G. O., *Syntax*. A Grammar of English Language in 3 vols. Vol. III. Boston, 1931.

DEUTSCHBEIN, M., *Neuenglische Stilistik*. Leipzig, 1932.

DORFLES, GILLO, *Communication and Symbol in the Work of Art*. The Journal of Aesthetics and Art Criticism, Vol. XV, No. 3, March 1957.

DUJARDIN, E., *Le monologue intérieur*. Son apparition, ses origines, sa place dans l'oeuvre de James Joyce. Paris, 1931.

ELIOT, T. S., *The Sacred Wood*. Essays on Poetry and Criticism. London, 1950 (1920).

EMPSON, WILLIAM, *Seven Types of Ambiguity*. London, 1953.

FAOLAIN, SEAN, *The Vanishing Hero*. Studies in Novelists of the Twenties. London, 1956.

FAULKNER, WILLIAM, *The Sound and the Fury*. New York, 1946.

FOERSTER, N., *The Impressionists*. The (American) Bookman, vol. LXX, 1929.

FOWLER, H. W., *A Dictionary of Modern English Usage*. Oxford, 1944.

FRIEDMAN, MELVIN, *Stream of Consciousness:* A Study in Literary Method. New Haven, 1955.

FROMM, ERICH, *The Forgotten Language*. An Introduction to the Understanding of Dreams, Fairy Tales and Myths. New York, 1951.

FRY, ROGER, *Vision and Design*. Harmondsworth, 1937 (1920).

GRAHAM, JOHN, *Time in the Novels of Virginia Woolf*. University of Toronto Quarterly, Vol. XVII, 1948—9.

GULLBERG, HELGE, *Berättarkonst och stil i Per Hallströms prosa*. Göteborg, 1939.

HAKULINEN, LAURI, *Sanojen sanottavaa*. Helsinki, 1958.

HAVARD-WILLIAMS, PETER AND MARGARET, *Bateau Ivre: The Symbol of the Sea in Virginia Woolf's The Waves*. English Studies 1953, Vol. 34, Nos. 1—6, Amsterdam—Bern—Copenhagen.

HEIDEGGER, MARTIN, *Sein und Zeit*. Tübingen, 1953.

HELLER, ERICH, *The Ironic German*. A Study of Thomas Mann. London, 1958.

—»— *The Realistic Fallacy*. The Listener, 19. 5. 1955.

Homén, Olof, *Poetik*. Helsingfors, 1953.

Jespersen, Otto, *Language*. Its Nature, Development and Origin. London, 1922.

—»— *Essentials of English Grammar*. London, 1956.

—»— *A Modern English Grammar VII*. Copenhagen, 1949.

Jung, C. G., *Contributions to Analytical Psychology*. London, 1942 (1928).

—»— *Modern Man in Search of a Soul*. New York, 1933.

Kayser, Wolfgang, *Das sprachliche Kunstwerk*. Bern u. München, 1959. (1948)

—»— *Die Vortragsreise*. Studien zur Literatur. Bern, 1958.

Keats, John, *Poetry and Prose*. Oxford, 1957.

Klages, Ludwig, *Vom Wesen des Rhythmus*. Kampen auf Sylt, 1943.

Koskimies, Rafael, *Theorie des Romans*. Helsinki, 1935.

—»— *Yleinen runousoppi*. Helsinki, 1949.

Kruisinga, E., *A Handbook of Present-day English, I—II*. Utrecht, 1925.

Langer, Susanne K., *Feeling and Form*. London, 1953.

—»— *Philosophy in a New Key*. New York, 1955 (1942).

Legouis, Émile, *A History of English Literature*. London, 1940 (1927).

Longinus, *On the Sublime*. Everyman's Library No. 901. London, 1953.

Louhija, Jarl, *Symbolit ja kielikuvat Bertel Gripenbergin tuotannossa*. Helsinki, 1959.

Lowes, J. Livingstone, *The Road to Xanadu*. London, 1927.

Luojola, Yrjö, *Ajan virta V. A. Koskenniemen runoudessa*. Valvoja No. 3, Helsinki, 1959.

Matson, Alex, *Muistiinpanoja*. Jyväskylä, 1959.

Matthiessen, F. O., *The Achievement of T. S. Eliot*. London, 1935.

Mayer, Felix, *Schöpferische Sprache und Rhythmus*. Berlin, 1959.

Murry, John Middleton, *The Problem of Style*. London, 1922.

—»— *Countries of the Mind*, ser. II. Essays in Literary Criticism. London, 1931.

—»— *Keats*. London, 1955.

Nieminen, K., *Juhani Ahon sanataide*. Tyylitutkimus. Porvoo, 1934.

Ogden G. K. & Richards, I. A., *The Meaning of Meaning*. London, 1944.

Ojala, Aatos, *Aestheticism and Oscar Wilde*. Part II. Literary Style. Helsinki, 1955.

Poe, E. A., *Tales, Poems, Essays*. Collins Classics. London & Glasgow, 1952.

Poutsma, H., *A Grammar of Late Modern English*. Groningen, 1905—28.

Press, John, *The Fire and the Fountain*. An Essay on Poetry. Oxford, 1955.

Ransom, John Crowe, *Poetry as Primitive Language*. The Writer and his Craft, ed. Ray W. Cowden. Ann Arbor, 1954.

Rantavaara, Irma, *Virginia Woolf and Bloomsbury*. Helsinki, 1953.

—»— *Romantic Imagery in Virginia Woolf's The Waves* with a Special Reference to Antithesis. Bulletin of the Modern Language Association, 1 LX, Helsinki, 1959.

—»— *Ing-forms in the service of rhythm and style in Virginia Woolf's The Waves*. Bulletin of the Modern Language Association, 1 LXI, Helsinki, 1960.

Read, Herbert, *English Prose Style*. London, 1928.

Reenpää, Yrjö, *Aufbau der allgemeinen Sinnesphysiologie*. Frankfurt am Main, 1959.

Richards, I. A., *Coleridge on Imagination*. London, 1934.

RICHARDS, I. A. *Speculative Instruments*. London, 1955.

RICHTER, ELISE, *Impressionismus, Expressionismus und Grammatik*. Zeitschrift für Romanische Philologie. Band XLVII, Halle a. S., 1927.

RYLANDS, GEORGE, *Words and Poetry*. London, 1928.

SHELLEY, PERCY BYSSHE, *The Poetical Works of*, London, 1949.

SEIDLER, HERBERT, *Die Dichtung*. Wesen-Form-Dasein. Stuttgart, 1959.

SPITZER, LEO, *Stilstudien I-II*. München, 1928.

—»— *Linguistics and Literary History*. Essays in Stylistics. Princeton, 1948.

STAIGER, EMIL, *Grundbegriff der Poetik*, Zürich, 1956 (1946).

—»— *Die Zeit als Einbildungskraft des Dichters*, Zürich, 1953.

—»— *Die Kunst der Interpretation*. Zürich, 1955.

THON, LUISE, *Die Sprache des deutschen Impressionismus*. München, 1928.

TINDALL WILLIAMS, *Forces in Modern British Literature* 1885—1956. New York, 1949 (1947).

TURNELL, MARTIN, *The Art of French Fiction*. London, 1959.

TUVE, ROSEMOND, *Elizabethan and Metaphysical Imagery*. Renaissance Poetic and Twentieth-century Critics. Chicago, 1947.

ULLMANN, STEPHEN, *Style in the French Novel*. Cambridge, 1957.

VALKAMA, LEEVI, *Tutkimus Johannes Linnankosken 'Pakolaisten' tyylistä*. Kokkola, 1957.

WALZEL, O., *Gehalt und Gestalt im Kunstwerk des Dichters*. Berlin, 1923.

—»— *Das Wortkunstwerk*. Leipzig, 1926.

WARREN, AUSTIN & WELLEK, RENÉ, *Theory of Literature*. London, 1954 (1949).

WILSON, EDMUND, *Legend and Symbol in Dr. Zhivago*. The Encounter, June 1959.

WEIDNER, EVA, *Impressionismus und Expressionismus in den Romanen Virginia Woolfs*. Berlin, 1934.

WIMSATT, WILLIAM, K. JR. & BROOKS, CLEANTH, *Literary Criticism*. A Short History. New York, 1957.

WORDSWORTH, WILLIAM, *The Prelude, or Growth of a Poet's Mind*. Ed. by Ernest de Selincourt (2 imp.), London, 1928.

ZANDVOORT, R. W., *A Handbook of English Grammar*. London, 1957.

INDEX